SITUATING EVERYDAY LIFE

SAGE has been part of the global academic community since 1965, supporting high quality research and learning that transforms society and our understanding of individuals, groups and cultures. SAGE is the independent, innovative, natural home for authors, editors and societies who share our commitment and passion for the social sciences.

Find out more at: **www.sagepublications.com**

SITUATING EVERYDAY LIFE
PRACTICES AND PLACES

SARAH PINK

SAGE

Los Angeles | London | New Delhi
Singapore | Washington DC

First published 2012

Apart from any fair dealing for the purposes of research or private study, or criticism or review, as permitted under the Copyright, Designs and Patents Act, 1988, this publication may be reproduced, stored or transmitted in any form, or by any means, only with the prior permission in writing of the publishers, or in the case of reprographic reproduction, in accordance with the terms of licences issued by the Copyright Licensing Agency. Enquiries concerning reproduction outside those terms should be sent to the publishers.

SAGE Publications Ltd
1 Oliver's Yard
55 City Road
London EC1Y 1SP

SAGE Publications Inc.
2455 Teller Road
Thousand Oaks, California 91320

SAGE Publications India Pvt Ltd
B 1/I 1 Mohan Cooperative Industrial Area
Mathura Road, Post Bag 7
New Delhi 110 044

SAGE Publications Asia-Pacific Pte Ltd
3 Church Street
#10-04 Samsung Hub
Singapore 049483

Library of Congress Control Number: 2011931561

British Library Cataloguing in Publication data

A catalogue record for this book is available from the British Library

ISBN 978-0-85702-056-7
ISBN 978-0-85702-057-4 (pbk)

Typeset by C&M Digitals (P) Ltd, Chennai, India
Printed by Replika Press Pvt. Ltd
Printed on paper from sustainable resources

CONTENTS

LIST OF FIGURES

ABOUT THE AUTHOR

Sarah Pink is Professor of Social Sciences at Loughborough University. Her research, rooted in anthropology and cognate social sciences engages across disciplines to connect with arts practice and applied agendas in design and engineering. In doing so she seeks to make connections between advances in theoretical scholarship, methodology and practical as well as academic research questions and themes. Her work most recently focuses on a range of everyday, activist and mediated contexts and processes, including questions about how these relate to everyday domestic life, digital media, energy, the construction industry and sustainability agendas. Most of her work engages visual and sensory methodologies and she has an enduring interest in the development of innovative methods. Her other books include *Home Truths* (2004), *The Future of Visual Anthropology* (2006), *Visual Interventions* (Editor) (2007), *Doing Visual Ethnography* (2007, 2nd edition), *Doing Sensory Ethnography* (2009), and *Advances in Visual Methodology* (2012).

ACKNOWLEDGEMENTS

This book is an outcome of a series of research projects that I have been involved in over a period of 10 or so years. It draws on and develops further ideas first presented in earlier work, including the books *Home Truths* (Pink 2004) and *Doing Sensory Ethnography* (Pink 2009a) as well as a good number of articles published between 2000 and 2011. Yet the synthesis and development of the materials, ideas and arguments developed in this book are new.

My first thanks, as always are to all the participants in my research who have given up their time to work with me, without them this book would have been impossible. Participation for those who have wished to be further involved meant not only taking part the ethnographic stage but also reading and commenting on some of the texts included in this book. I will not mention everyone by name here since some have preferred to remain anonymous and those who have not are named in the chapters where our collaborations are discussed. I am similarly grateful to the organisations that have funded the ethnographic research projects discussed in this book, and colleagues and friends who have commented on the various chapters, as follows.

Chapter 4 is based on research undertaken as part of a study titled *Cleaning, Homes and Lifestyles* undertaken with Unilever Research in 1999, with Katie Deverell. I am grateful to both Unilever and the staff I collaborated with there, for their support in this work. Chapter 5 is also based on research done with Unilever Research, in 2000, as part of a study about the use of laundry tablets in the UK, with Jean Rimmer at Unilever and in collaboration with Marie Corbin. I would also like to thank Nicki Morley of Unilever Research for her support at this publication stage. Much of the inspiration for re-thinking laundry through questions of energy and sustainability has, however, come from my work with colleagues in design and engineering at Loughborough University, and I would also like to acknowledge the influence of this environment on my work.

Chapters 6 and 7 are based on research funded initially by the Faculty of Social Sciences and Humanities at Loughborough University and following this by a small grant from the Nuffield Foundation. Chapter 6 was first presented as a keynote lecture at the conference 'Home and urbanity: cultural perspectives on housing and everyday life' organised by the Center for Housing and Welfare, Copenhagen University in 2008. I am very grateful to the organisers of the conference for giving me the opportunity to present my work at this event and to the conference participants whose comments on my paper and with whom I discussed its ideas have helped me to develop it into its present form. Elements of Chapter 7 were originally published in 'Urban Social Movements and Small Places' in the journal *City* (Pink 2009b) although these have been re-worked in this book, and the section entitled 'Histories, memories and biographies: the personal and the collective in Cittaslow carnival' was previously published in a slightly different form in an article titled 'Amateur documents?: amateur photographic practice, collective representation and the constitution of place in UK slow cities' in *Visual Studies* (2011b). I would also like to thank Cittaslow Aylsham, Aylsham Town Council, Broadland District Council and Norfolk County Council for permissions to publish the images included in Chapter 7 (credits are included in the figure captions). My warmest thanks also go to those past and present members of the Cittaslow committees in UK member towns, who have maintained a continuing interest in support of my work.

Chapter 8 was written during my sabbatical leave from the Department of Social Sciences at Loughborough University in 2010–11. I am very grateful to the University for this time to focus on my research, during which I was a Visiting Scholar at the Internet Interdisciplinary Institute (IN3) at the Universitat Oberta de Catalunya in Barcelona. I would like to thank the IN3 for hosting my work during this academic year and providing a stimulating intellectual environment in which to develop my ideas about the practices and places of digital and social media. I am also grateful to Andrea Mearns, the Cittaslow International Committee UK Representative, for generously reading and commenting on my discussion of the movement's online presence and to John Postill for his several readings of and comments on this chapter as it developed.

Finally, I would also like to thank Karen O'Reilly and Lydia Martens for giving up their time to read and comment on Chapter 4 at an earlier stage of the development of this work, to Francesco Lapenta who read and commented on the first draft of the manuscript, to SAGE's anonymous reviewer, and to Chris Rojek and Jai Seaman at SAGE.

1

INTRODUCTION: (RE)THINKING ABOUT EVERYDAY LIFE AND ACTIVISM

In a contemporary context, the sustainability agendas of governments, activists and ordinary people inevitably involve the production of new relationships between the material and sensory environments and activities that constitute the everyday. In this book I explore how concepts of place and practice can be engaged to further our understandings of the environments and activities of everyday life through an exploration of domestic consumption, sustainability and activism. The theoretical tools of practice and place, I argue, are particularly important for this task – since together they provide us with analytical routes to understanding both human activity and the environment. Indeed in seeking to understand how we might work towards achieving environmental sustainability, the questions of how practices and places are constituted, how they change and shift over time, or how they are maintained are pertinent for scholars and applied researchers across different sectors and academic disciplines.

Situating Everyday Life examines how processes of renewal and change are lived, experienced and represented through a series of everyday and mediated research contexts. I examine questions relating to why and how we live in ways that sometimes unnecessarily consume energy and other resources and how some people are seeking to make changes that will make the everyday worlds they live in more environmentally sustainable. To do this I draw on a series of different ethnographic and digital research projects undertaken during the past decade or so to examine progressively how domestic lives, local community projects, urban identities and digital media and web platforms are bound up with the flows and movements through which change happens.

For this task an approach that is inevitably interdisciplinary is needed. This is in part because the existing literatures that focus on everyday life, the theoretical approaches to practice and place, and the contexts in which these understandings have potential practical applications, span a number of disciplines. For example, while interest in the study of everyday life originated in the social sciences, arts and humanities, its relevance is now far more wide-ranging. It is increasingly being recognised that social science understandings of the everyday practices and places where technologies are used, change happens and resources are consumed are important for other fields of science. Design and engineering interventions that focus on questions of sustainability, climate change, creating environments for wellbeing, and more, also require understandings of everyday contexts and lives. Moreover, areas of sustainability and climate change are precisely where the concerns of activists, governments and academics are tending to coincide. The approach I take here is inter-disciplinary in that it attends to the ways that everyday life research has emerged from different scholarly traditions. It moreover draws from existing arguments developed in philosophy, anthropology, sociology and geography to respond to three contemporary theoretical strands that have been referred to as the 'sensorial turn' (Howes 2003: xii) or 'sensory turn' (Edwards et al. 2006: 11), the 'practice turn' (Schatzki et al. 2001) and the 'spatial turn' (see Hubbard et al. 2004: 2). I propose that by bringing together these approaches an understanding that is sensitive to both the politics and phenomenology of everyday realities and processes of change is possible.

PRACTICES AND PLACES

Given that the interest in everyday life and activism as sites for change and routes to transformation is interdisciplinary and crosses scholarly and applied research, there is all the more need for a coherent and encompassing route to both researching and theorising them. Because everyday life and activism are implicated in wider processes we need to account for the relationship between the activities and environments in which they are played out. We moreover need to recognise that our activities as researchers are likewise a part of these same environments. Chapters 2 and 3 of this book undertake this task by proposing a theoretical and methodological agenda for understanding everyday life, activist and research processes through a set of theoretical principles that are under-pinned by an understanding of the relationship of practices and places as mutually constituting. In Chapter 2, I undertake a critical exploration of existing theories of practice and place. Practice, I argue – whether one is concerned with the practices of domestic cleaning, community gardening, creating a public activist event or posting on Facebook – is essentially neither resistant nor normative. Rather, it needs to be understood as open to being a source of potential for the production of change, for maintaining things apparently as they are or for simultaneously doing both in different ways. Moreover, practices cannot be understood as being performed in isolation from the wider environments of which they are a part. Therefore I propose that a theory of place is needed, that can offer us a way of understanding how the diverse components that constitute the contingency of any environment in which everyday and activist practices are actually lived and experienced. Here, following recent developments in theorising place in geography and anthropology, I argue that place should be understood as an abstract concept and as distinct from locality. Yet, as I show, we also need to attend to the ways in which people create and experience a 'sense of place' in relation to material localities. In Chapter 3, I reflect on how one might go about learning about everyday life and activism as they are lived out in practice and in place. Insisting on theoretical coherence between the way we understand research practice and findings, I explore how theoretical understandings of place and practice lead us to an appreciation of how human action is always situated in relation to specific environmental, material, sensory, social and discursive configurations, and how we might comprehend representations from this perspective.

This book is written in the context of an increasing focus on the senses in contemporary scholarship, whereby it has been acknowledged that attention to the senses is central to the analysis of practice (e.g. Ingold 2000, Sutton 2006, Grasseni 2007, Marchand 2007) and place (e.g. Feld and Basso 1996, Pink 2009a). Indeed, the senses have long since figured in the work of twentieth-century scholars of everyday life (Gardiner 2000), including Benjamin, Lefebvre and de Certeau (Highmore 2002), anthropologists (e.g. Stoller 1989, Howes 1991, Seremetakis 1994) and geographers (e.g. Tuan 1993, Rodaway 1994). Yet contemporary theoretical developments also imply new ways of understanding sensory perception. The approach to the senses in this book unites an understanding of the multisensoriality of methodological process (Pink 2009a) with an understanding of empirical contexts. This involves departing from the modern Western understanding of the five-sense sensorium whereby our common sense tells us we simply smell through our noses, hear through our ears and see through our eyes. Rather, building on both the phenomenology of perception and neurological studies, the senses can be understood as interconnected, and at the level of perception inseparable. Ingold (2000) has effectively brought the philosophy of Maurice Merleau-Ponty and the ecological psychology of James Gibson together to emphasise the inseparability of these sensory categories in processes of perception. This assumes that the way we know the world is not dominated by any one sense (see also Ingold 2000) but involves a much less clearly defined mixture of sense experience that is classified into cultural categories. Indeed ethnographic research has demonstrated that the range and types of sensory categories used to describe multisensory embodied experiences may vary in different contexts. Outside modern Western contexts, it has been most clearly noticeable that the five-sense sensorium is culturally constructed and not a universal classificatory system (see, for example, Geurts 2002 for a discussion of this). Equally, recent work by neurologists suggests that understandings based on the idea of differentially sensing modalities attached to specific sense organs should be replaced by understandings of the senses as interconnected in human perception – in that 'the five senses do not travel along separate channels, but interact to a degree few scientists would have believed only a decade ago' (Cytowic 2010: 46, see also discussion of this in Pink 2009a). These developments not only call on researchers to attend to the senses when seeking to understand how other people live and act in the world. They also invite us to attend to the multisensory and embodied ways in which environments are experienced and the unspoken, the tacit and the ways of knowing and communicating in everyday life and activist practice that are not verbalised. As I show in the following chapters, attention to multisensoriality has theoretical and methodological implications, leading us on new routes to understanding the practices and places of everyday life and activism.

EVERYDAY LIFE AND ACTIVISM: ESTABLISHING CONTINUITIES

Everyday life and activism are often studied in isolation from each other. The everyday has tended to be associated with the mundane, the routine and the hidden or at least unnoticed. Activism in contrast has been linked to the public, explicit, explosive and sometimes even glamorous elements of political life. The contrast is even starker when we consider how everyday domestic life has in the past often been framed as a site of women's oppression coupled with hidden forms of resistance, while activism is associated with explicit power relations, public campaigns and protest such as direct action. Yet while the fact that these types of power relations are indeed experienced in some contexts, such dichotomies are increasingly being revealed as irrelevant – in both theory and experience. This is particularly so in relation to the context I address in this book, characterised by the growth of activist movements and the increasing number of ordinary people working towards sustainability agendas, often in tandem with governments and businesses. Indeed it is possible to understand everyday life as a site that has equal potential for activist practices as those of a global political arena. Although of course these practices and the places of which they are part will be different. Further continuities between the sites and practices of activism and everyday life are also established through contemporary developments in what has been called Web 2.0, social media web platforms and their potential for communications and campaigning. These questions and connections are addressed as we move through Chapters 4 to 8. Yet there is significant background to the study of both everyday life and activism across the social sciences and humanities.

The endless unfolding of everyday life, its aesthetics, emotions, experiences, environments and politics has long since fascinated scholars, writers and artists. It is the domain of activity that the interventions of many policy makers, designers and engineers seek to reach. It is where we make our worlds and where our worlds make us. Therefore everyday life is a context of human creativity, innovation and change, and a site where processes towards a sustainable future might be initiated and nurtured. It is moreover, subsequently a locus from which and in which contemporary concerns about environment and sustainability might be addressed. Likewise the study of activism, social movements and political leaders has been a part of the history of the social sciences. It also involves sets of practices and processes that are inevitably both experiential at a personal level, embodied and social as well as political and intended to lead to forms of change. Environmental activism is moreover a starting point from which some movements are seeking to work towards a sustainable future, in ways that implicate both policy and everyday life practices. By considering everyday life and activism together, we can begin to see that activism has implications for everyday life, while at the same time, doing activism is itself an everyday life activity, often performed in environments such as homes, gardens or local neighbourhoods. Existing understandings emerging from everyday life studies often comprehend the everyday as a site for resistance. If we refigure this focus on resistance as a starting point for understanding the everyday as a site for change and for activism, the politics of the everyday might be recast. The activist practices of both social movement campaigners and the innovations of everyday life practitioners are situated within the context of local and global flows, and are part of wider material, sensory, social and mediated environments, or ecologies of things, media, processes, discourses and biographies.

In this book, building on and departing from existing trends in researching everyday life through paradigms of practice, materiality and text, and researching activism through paradigms of network, I propose a shift towards understanding both everyday life and activism in terms of practices and places. The novelty of this approach is that it combines three key principles: it allows a focus on how the detail of everyday life and activism are enacted and experienced, thus moving away from the study of everyday life and activism as involving sets of practices to a focus on the phenomenology of everyday life and activism *in* practice; it understands everyday life and activism both as always part of and co-constitutive of specific environmental configurations, thus suggesting that neither actually happen *in* places but rather that everyday life and activism are implicated in the making of places in unique combination with other processes; and it understands the persons, representations and material culture of everyday life and of activism as always being in movement. While the study of the phenomenology, politics and representations of everyday life and activist practices and places are not in themselves new, these approaches tend to have been developed in different disciplines and for different purposes.

In the following two sections of this introduction I situate the contribution of this book in relation to some key relevant strands in the study of everyday life and activism and the issues they raise. In doing so I suggest that attending more closely to questions emerging at the interrelationship between practice and place may bring new insights to both fields of scholarship.

EVERYDAY LIFE STUDIES AND THE STUDY OF EVERYDAY LIFE

Various layers of historical and contemporary scholarship and arts practice exist around everyday life. A number of contemporary scholars, such as Michael Gardiner (2000, 2009), Ben Highmore (2002) and Michael Sheringham (2006) critically discuss and synthesise the work of twentieth-century theorists and artists of everyday life. Collectively their discussions already imply the interdisciplinarity of twentieth-century everyday life studies, for example through the sociology of Georg Simmel, the anthropology of Michel de Certeau, the philosophy of Henri Lefebvre, and their interest in surrealist art. Yet, these existing approaches to interdisciplinarity are largely historical rather than pursuing the implications of the themes they identify through to contemporary disciplinary and/or interdisciplinary trajectories to consider how geographers, sociologists or anthropologists have since understood everyday life through ethnographic research. There subsequently seems to be something of a gulf between cultural studies and other social science and humanities approaches to everyday life. For example in cultural studies, Highmore has suggested that the everyday life theory he discusses is 'an invitation to start thinking about an area of life that manages, for the most part to avoid scrutiny' (2002: vii) and Joe Moran has announced that his own book 'aims to show that the spaces and practice of modern daily life were not always boring or routine' (2005: 26). Taking into consideration the increasing number of publications that approach everyday life from a theoretical or cultural studies perspective already cited above, since Highmore's (2002) comments, it could be said that the point is already out of date. Yet, casting the interdisciplinary net wider it becomes clear that the everyday simply does not 'avoid scrutiny' (Highmore 2002: iv). For example, for over a century social anthropologists have researched the detail of other people's lives in developing countries and for much of this period have also focused similar attention on modern Western contexts. As ethnographers they have systematically learned to live with and learn from other people precisely by sharing aspects of their everyday lives. Scholars in European ethnology have even focused on some of the very same issues and questions that preoccupy cultural studies scholars of everyday life. For example, in British cultural studies Moran (2005) focuses on waiting and commuting, while in Sweden, ethnologists Orvar Löfgren and Billy Ehn (2010) focus on waiting, routines and daydreaming and Tom O'Dell (2010) works on spas and commuting. Sociologists (e.g. Casey and Martens 2007, Shove et al. 2007, 2009) have also engaged through qualitative research in the detail of other people's everyday experiences – in a number of public and domestic domains. The deficiency is therefore not that everyday life was not already a key area of research – indeed internationally. Rather it is that there has been little joining up of these bodies of work theoretically or empirically. The study of the theory of everyday life and of its representations in literature and art are often undertaken in isolation from the ethnographic and qualitative literature on everyday life. One of the tasks of this book is to seek to make connections between these approaches.

This absence of connection is reflected further in that in the work of ethnographers the term everyday life often tends to refer to an assumed or uninterrogated category. For many contemporary anthropologists and sociologists, everyday life is a given; it is not a neglected domain of practice that needs to be brought to the fore, or a category that needs to be defined. Rather it is part of the substantive focus that they seek to understand when they research other people's lives and develop their analyses in relation to alternative theoretical paradigms. For example, take three recent texts which relate to themes that are pertinent to this book and have the term everyday life in their titles. My own monograph about gender and the sensory home is titled *Home Truths: Gender, Domestic Objects and Everyday Life* (2004). There I use the notion of everyday life as a category for referring to the way life is lived out in the home on an everyday basis in the form of practices of home decoration and housework, and my ethnographic concerns were precisely with the question of how and why everyday life is lived as it is and the details of the sensory and affective experiences of home. My theoretical concerns were with developing the notion of the sensory home and to explore changing gender performances and identities within this framework – rather than an engagement with theories of everyday life. In their book *The Design of Everyday Life* (2007), Elizabeth Shove, Matthew Watson, Martin Hand and Jack Ingram refer to the 'vast amount of scholarship' that sociologists and anthropologists have paid to the materiality of everyday life (2007: 2) and moreover make a systematic attempt to analyse and understand 'the ongoing dynamics of everyday life' (2007: 11). Yet theoretically their analysis is rooted in sociological approaches to consumption, the practice theory of Theodore Schatzki and Bruno Latour's ideas concerning materiality. Therefore, while its authors undoubtedly engage with questions about the practices of everyday life, *The Design of Everyday Life* makes connections and critical interventions across disciplinary fields by developing a theoretical and practical agenda that links with design studies. Finally, Gerard Goggin's *Cell Phone Culture: Mobile Technology in Everyday Life* (2006) draws on two key theoretical strands. The first is the cultural studies notion of the 'circuit of culture' (2006: 6), through which he suggests that 'It is fitting then that we study the cell phone to understand the modernities in which we are placed now' (2006: 8). The second is Latour's actor network theory, drawing from which he proposes that 'In appreciating the development and histories of cell phones, we will need to attend to the many people and things these devices have enlisted and to follow these actors as these technologies unfold' (Goggin 2006: 12). Goggin is certainly interested in what people do with cell phones [mobile phones], and it is easy to move from the mention of everyday life in the subtitle of his book to surmise that indeed everyday life practices are the stuff of 'cell phone culture'. Yet again we see the study of everyday life moving in a new theoretical direction. These points invite a question: has the *concept* of 'everyday life', or its interrogation for its own sake, become redundant to qualitative sociologists, anthropologists, human geographers and media scholars? While, in contrast, for cultural studies scholars focusing instead on representations of everyday life culture (e.g. Highmore 2002, Moran 2005), the concept itself remains central.

Scholars who are actually researching and/or writing about the practices, technologies and localities through which life is lived and indeed through which culture is produced are tending to reconceptualise everyday life through alternative theoretical approaches, while also accounting for its relevance to specific substantive themes and questions. In the following chapters I follow this trend, by arguing that everyday life is appropriately understood through a theory of practice and place.

INDIRECT ACTIVISM, THE URBAN AND THE EVERYDAY

The study of activism is, like everyday life scholarship, a field of inter-disciplinary concern. Most relevant for the discussion in this book are recent contributions from geography, sociology and anthropology, with particular emphasis on questions of urban activism. Indeed, in recent years, urban social movements and academic approaches to them have changed since the initial surge of scholarship in this area in the 1970s and 1980s in ways that make them very relevant both for the field of everyday life studies and for understanding the rela-tionship of activist practices to particular environments. Moreover, more recently as digital and social media activism takes on new sig-nificance, it is increasingly becoming a key field for analysis at the intersections between these disciplines and media studies.

There is a general sense in which urban social movements are becoming more integrated in existing social structures, and it is this aspect of the development of contemporary activism that I am concerned with in this book. For instance, Lila Leontidou highlights how among urban social movements increasingly legalised and officially recognised uses of urban spaces are now emerging (Leontidou 2006) and Margit Mayer notes a tendency for 'state programmes [to] ... now partner with movement organisations even as the latter seek to implement their own visions of a social economy, empowerment, sustainable neighbourhoods, etc.' (2006: 203). This contemporary approach to urban activism invites us to consider how through ideologically informed appropriations of urban localities activists generate the conditions for particular everyday life experiences and practices. The processes of legalisation and state recognition of urban social movements also invite us to rethink how activism can be implicated in processes of change. It is not necessarily the state as a total institution that such urban social movements resist, but certain flows of, for instance, global corporate capitalism. Thus urban social movements are increasingly connected to, influenced by and indeed *influential in* state and government bodies. In this book I focus on this type of activism as it is developed in towns and through digital media. The Cittaslow (slow city) movement, discussed in Chapters 6–8, is characteristic of these changes. Cittaslow (although sometimes precariously) becomes embedded in town councils and has also attracted the interest of regional councils (Pink 2009b). It offers an example of how a very contemporary style of activism for a sustainability agenda is played out. Such forms of activism are also particularly interesting because they cannot be studied in ways that are separated from the study of everyday life. This is because Cittaslow and similar movements impact on the material and sensory environments of towns, and extend the potentials these hold for practices that local people might engage in. They are inevitably concerned with everyday life as a site for change and thus have implications for domestic consumption practices.

At the same time, attending to forms of activism that are produced by internationally networked movements and concerned with global change reminds us that attention to context also implies a global and political domain. The sociologist Manuel Castells has identified the global–local nexus as essential to the capacity of urban social movements to engender change. Indeed he cautions that by 'enclosing themselves in their communities, urban social movements may contribute to further spatial fragmentation, ultimately to the breakdown of society' (Castells 2002 [2000]: 396). But, conversely 'by reaching out to the cultural transformation of urban life as proposed by ecological thinkers and activists … urban social movements can transcend their limits of localism' (Castells 2002 [2000]: 396). This global-local nexus is crucial for the example of Cittaslow activism and its analysis enables us to understand how local practices and configurations of place are implicated in wider processes of change. Interpreted through a theory of 'place beyond place' (Massey 2007) the activist and everyday practices that Cittaslow engenders can be seen as being simultaneously local and global. Therefore the localities where activist projects are created become both the intersections of complex sets of power relations and frame the experienced realities where people live out their everyday lives. In my existing work I have stressed the sensory socialities of activism (Pink 2008b) and how activist practices can create a phenomenology of place that offers alternative sensory embodied experiences (Pink 2009a). In Chapters 6–8 I develop these themes by progressively focusing on a series of interconnected domains to analyse: how a neighbourhood project is created by local people but within an activist frame, how urban environments are constituted through activist practices and the ways that mediated activism is practised on the Internet.

CONTEXTS FOR SUSTAINABILITY

In this book the concept of sustainability is broadly conceived, in that I am concerned with sets of issues and practices including those that work towards, for example, using less fossil fuel energy, reducing carbon emissions in domestic homes and in towns, the distribution and consumption of local produce, creating green spaces, and adherence to Local Agenda 21.

Each chapter focuses on a different environment ranging from the kitchen, the home, the neighbourhood, the town to the Internet, all of which are contexts through which sustainability agendas may be pursued. These examples have been selected to progressively show how the theoretical tools of practice and place enable us to understand how innovation, change and activism develop across a range of different contexts. Each chapter also takes a different focus to bring to the fore a specific element of the ways in which we might understand everyday life through theories of practice and place. Therefore, Chapter 4 focuses on the detail of how individual performances of kitchen practices are contingent on configurations of place and individual biographies and identities. This analysis, I suggest, can enable us to understand how individual practitioners are implicated in the innovative processes through which energy-consuming practices come about, and moreover demonstrates the importance of situating these performances as part of specific environments. Chapter 5 foregrounds the question of how the movements and flows of things and persons implicated in a particular practice is involved in creating and responds to the sensory aesthetics and social relations of the domestic environment. Here I show how by following people and things in movement, we are able to learn about the intersections between things that both create the 'feel' of the home, and are simultaneously influential in determining how domestic energy is consumed. In Chapter 6, the focus moves on to a new context – the neighbourhood. Here my focus is on the development of a community garden project, which is framed by the work of the Cittaslow movement. In this example the interrelations between the practices of local people – of imagining, gardening and walking – intersect with global flows including the global principles of an urban social movement and donations from global businesses. The chapter shows how by focusing on flows and practices that extend through the garden, we are able to understand how an everyday place and the experiences that local residents have of it are transformed in a sustainable way. Chapter 7 focuses more directly on the work of the Cittaslow movement as I shift the analysis to the level of the town. Here I am concerned with the ways in which a sustainable urban environment is created through the projects of activists through town council policies and festive events. As I show, an analysis of how activist practices constitute particular types of urban environments (some longer term than others) enables us to see how new possibilities for everyday life activities, experiences and routines that respond to a sustainability agenda are made for local residents. Finally, in Chapter 8, I examine how the Internet can be understood as an environment that is both part of everyday life and integral to the work of sustainability activism. Here I move the analytical emphasis further towards a focus on how a theory of place can be applied to understanding the mediated environments that form part of the everyday lives of many people. I analyse the website and the Cittaslow international blog, YouTube channel, photography and news and events items to argue that these configurations of genres and media can be understood as potential constituents of place.

As should be clear by now, the aim of this book is to make an argument and to demonstrate an analytical route through which we might come to understand how individuals and environments influence the possibilities for sustainable everyday living. Each chapter presents an example that works with the same theoretical approaches of practice and place, yet offers a different entry point into the analysis. As such this book is not intended to present a holistic empirical report that demonstrates through a single case study how sustainability might be achieved and why it is sometimes not. Rather it is an analysis of interrelated examples that have been selected precisely to show how different activities and environments might be comprehended and thus studied as part of sustainability research.

FOR A NEW PERSPECTIVE ON EVERYDAY LIFE AND ACTIVISM: TO CONCLUDE

In sum, it is my hope that the reader of this book will start to re-think the everyday and activism as sites with the potential for change, from a perspective that attends to the environments and activities through which life is lived, and with the recognition that she or he is also right in the middle of this world. As I outline in the next two chapters, this means theorising and researching everyday life as something we are inevitably *in*. By this I mean we are both in the flow of everyday life, of being and doing, and we are in and part of the very environments of everyday life. To understand everyday life as both a source of activism and change, as well as a domain where sustainability might be achieved,

I argue that we need to comprehend it from within — rather than by seeking to extract data about it to analyse somewhere else, to read it as if it were text or to try to read it from texts. It is through a theory of practice and place that we can comprehend the material, social, sensory and mediated environments of which everyday life, activism and thus processes through which sustainability might be achieved, all form a part.

2

THEORISING THE FAMILIAR: PRACTICES AND PLACES

This chapter focuses on the theoretical tools needed to understand both how everyday life is constituted and experienced, and the consequences that the living of everyday life has for the environments of which it is part. The existing literature indicates that the study of the relationship between mind, body and environment is essential to this task, as are concepts of knowing, movement and sensing. Moreover, as I have stressed in Chapter 1, to understand everyday life we need to acknowledge that it is neither static nor necessarily mundane, and to understand activism we need to recognise that it not only involves dramatic public actions but is also embedded in ordinary ways of being. Both everyday life and activism are located in, and indeed part of, dynamic and changing material, sensory and social environments, and shifting ways of perceiving, knowing and being. Furthermore, from the outset, we should recognise that everyday life is also what we are currently engaged in, as researchers, writers and readers. In the case of activist scholars moreover, research and its representation is a form of intervention. Indeed, for all scholars, research constitutes a way to critically intervene, and as such to make change. Therefore, living life and making interventions are not detached from what and who we are – they are processes we are part of.

Place and practice, the two key concepts I work with in this book, are and have long since been important in theoretical debate in the social sciences and humanities. They have also been frequently used to understand the ways we live everyday life and how processes of change come about. Yet they are used across disciplines and substantive areas in ways that are contested, debated and often inconsistent. Because the terms practice and place are moreover frequently used labels in non-academic languages, there is also a tendency for their lay and academic uses to be conflated. Thus their purposes as abstract ways of conceptualising complex configurations of things or activities can become confused with discussions or even simply descriptions of actual localities or actions leading to confusion between analytical and local categories. Furthermore, terms that in one text refer to theoretical concepts in another might be used in a purely descriptive sense. In this chapter I propose a route through these literatures. This is not intended to be a full review of the diverse array of twentieth- and twenty-first century thought on practice and place. Rather, through a focus on key contributors and influences in recent debates about practice and place, I explore how we might understand these two processes in a way that constructs a coherent relationship between them.

Before proceeding however, I wish to stress that the theoretical concerns of this book should be understood as routes both to and from ethnographic knowing. They are *routes to* ethnographic knowing in that they are being used to make ethnographic findings meaningful and coherent. Yet simultaneously they are *routes from* ethnographic knowing in that the theoretical route taken here was developed in response to the findings of ethnographic research undertaken over a period of around 10 years. As the practice theorist Andreas Reckwitz reminds us: 'practice theory is not "true" (in the sense of corresponding to the "facts"), nor are the other versions of social and cultural theory "false" (or vice versa). After all, social theories are vocabularies necessarily underdetermined by empirical "facts"' (2002: 257). The same applies to theories of place, which likewise do not represent any objective truth. Indeed, geographers point to great diversity in how notions of space and place have been used (Hubbard et al. 2004: 6). Yet both are routes that allow us to enter, at an abstract level, a world of social and environmental realities and imaginings, and are thus a basis from which to understand our encounters in them.

In the first part of this chapter, I examine how theories of practice have been engaged in the analysis of everyday life and have been used to explain processes of change. I suggest that while such approaches provide an important route through which to approach and comprehend human activity in the world, they benefit from being further situated. For this purpose a theory of place offers us a way to understand how practices are co-constituted through a wider ecology of processes, and it is to this I turn in the second part of the chapter.

APPROACHING THE WORLD THROUGH PRACTICES

Concepts of practice are at the heart of a number of twentieth- and twenty-first century discussions of everyday life. The term practice, however, tends to be used in academic writing in two ways. First, it is frequently used as a descriptive term that refers to things people do, but with no real attention to its theoretical or abstract implications. In this use the term is not applied as an analytical concept, and should not be taken as such. Second, and especially in the context of what has been called the 'practice turn' (Schatzki et al. 2001) in contemporary thinking, practices have come to be defined, loosely, as sets of human actions that can be associated with each other in some way and that can form a category for sociological analysis. Therefore, for instance, we might refer to practices of washing up, doing the laundry, gardening, digital photography and social media activism. Yet in the existing literatures theories of practice and the uses they have been put to are diverse (Schatzki 2001, Postill 2010) – meaning there is 'no unified practice approach' (Schatzki 2001: 2). John Postill has suggested understanding the development of practice theory in terms of the work of two generations of practice theorists. The first includes thinkers such as Bourdieu (e.g. 1977) and de Certeau (1984, de Certeau et al. 1998), and has been a focus on interest for scholars of everyday life theory, especially in cultural studies. The second generation centres around the work of Schatzki (1996, 2001), Reckwitz (2002) and others (see Postill 2010: 6) and has been an inspiration for sociologists of consumption and sustainability. In this first part of the chapter I focus on three issues: the different ways that first and second generation practice theories have been engaged in everyday life studies and in the sociology of consumption; the question of the individual practitioner; and the situating of practices in relation to other elements and processes. In doing so I examine the potential of a concept of practice as an entry point for understanding everyday life and activism.

RECONSIDERING PRACTICE AND RESISTANCE

In some literatures a debate has emerged concerning the extent to which the practices of everyday life have potential for the generation of resistance, following the theory of Michel de Certau, or the maintenance of normativity associated with the work of Pierre Bourdieu. These different approaches represent rather different understandings of the potential, nature and essential qualities and potentials of practice, and in this section I provide a brief analysis of the debate for three purposes: first, for the practical reason that the ideas of de Certeau and Bourdieu continue to be highly influential across the social sciences and humanities, and readers are likely to encounter them in other literatures concerning everyday life and the politics and spatialities of domestic and urban contexts; second, because the debate reveals a difference between the interests of scholars of everyday life studies discussed in Chapter 1 and those of sociologists of consumption discussed in the next section; and third, the debate brings to the fore notions of normativity and resistance and thus questions relating to the idea of everyday life as a site for change.

Michel De Certeau's *The Practice of Everyday Life* (1984, de Certeau et al. 1998) celebrates everyday life as a site for resistance and appropriation, and as such appeals to the field of everyday life scholarship that seeks to 'rescue the everyday from the neglect and oblivion to which it is customarily consigned' (Sheringham 2006: 1, see also Moran 2005: 26). For Gardiner, de Certeau's approach has an 'ethical quality' since 'he draws our attention to the "symbolic violence" that can be done to the integrity of daily practices and to "otherness" under the guise of a systematic theoretical understanding of social reality' (2000: 179) and Giard highlights his belief in 'the *truant freedom of practices*' (original italics) and perception of 'microdifferences where so many others see obedience and standardisation' (Giard 1998c: xxii).

De Certeau's understanding of everyday life practices focuses on the activities of people as 'consumers' who navigate, appropriate and 'poach' in the face of the 'systems' of power (1984: xvii). This relation between the weak and the powerful is characterised by their respective use of 'tactics' and 'strategies'. A strategy involves 'the calculation (or manipulation) of power relationships that becomes possible as soon as a subject with will and power (a business, an army, a city, a scientific institution) can be isolated'; it signifies ownership over and management of a 'place' and a basis of power (1984: 35–6). A tactic by contrast 'is a calculated action determined by the absence of a proper locus', it is played out in 'the space of the other' and 'Thus it must play on and with the terrain imposed on it and organised by the law of a foreign power'. It is 'an art of the weak' (1984: 37) that involves being opportunistic, mobile and making 'use of the cracks that particular conjunctions open in the surveillance of the proprietary powers' (1984: 37) and is characterised by the 'absence of power' (1984: 38). The perpetrator of tactics operates the 'art of putting one over on the adversary on his own turf, hunter's tricks, manoeuvrable, polymorph mobilities, jubilant, poetic, and warlike discoveries' (1984: 40).

In contrast Bourdieu (who developed his theory of practice largely to refute arguments that human behaviour was driven by economic rationality [Bourdieu in Bourdieu and Wacquant 1992: 120]) argued that practices were precognitive, embedded in what he referred to as 'habitus' – meaning 'a *structuring mechanism* that operates from within agents' who internalise 'external structures'. While the habitus is 'neither strictly individual nor in itself fully determinative of conduct', it provided an explanation for the regularity and predictability of social life (Wacquant in Bourdieu and Wacquant 1992: 18, original italics); thus offering a framework for understanding normativity. The habitus was situated as dependent on both external elements and on practitioners. Externally it is structured by what Bourdieu refers to as the 'field', which he defined as 'a configuration of objective relations between position'. Different fields have different 'logics' (Bourdieu in Bourdieu and Wacquant 1992: 98), which might be explained in that each field 'follows rules or, better regularities, that are not explicit and codified' (Bourdieu in Bourdieu and Wacquant 1992: 99). Habitus is both structured by the field and 'contributes to constituting the field as a meaningful world, a world endorsed with sense and value, in which it: is worth investing one's energy' (Bourdieu and Wacquant 1992: 127). To explain the actions of individuals within this world of precognitive and externally structured behaviour, Bourdieu developed the concept of *illusio* to refer to 'the various forms of hidden, nonmaterial profits that guide agents who appear "disinterested"' and 'to convey the idea that people are motivated, driven by, torn from a state of indifference and moved by the stimuli sent by certain fields – and not others' (Wacquant in Bourdieu and Wacquant 1992: 26). As Bourdieu puts it: 'Each field calls forth and gives life to a specific form of interest, a specific *illusio*, as tacit recognition of the value of the stakes of the game and as practical mastery of its rules. Furthermore, this specific interest implied by one's participation in the game differentiates itself according to the position occupied in the game … and with the trajectory that leads each participant to this position' (Bourdieu in Bourdieu and Wacquant 1992: 117); thus explaining why different actors might navigate the field in different ways.

Everyday life scholars sharply distinguish de Certeau's approach from that of Bourdieu in that, as Sheringham puts it, 'unlike the tactics of Certeau, the practices studied by Bourdieu are not free and active but serve ultimately, albeit indirectly to bolster established structures' (2006: 215). Thus characterising de Certeau's idea of practice as 'productive' (Sheringham 2006: 213) whereas 'Bourdieu's logic of practices is based on reproduction rather than production' (Sheringham 2006: 215) and corresponding with de Certeau's assertion that Bourdieu 'proceeds to imprison these devices [i.e. what for de Certeau would be tactics] behind the bars of the unconscious' (1984: 60). However, the celebration of de Certeau as against Bourdieu has some limits. First, because the attribution of a rigid brand of determinism to Bourdieu's work has been framed as a misinterpretation (see Bourdieu and Wacquant 1992: 135–6). Second, because de Certeau does not clearly identify the source of the forms of tactic and resistance that he argues characterise everyday life practice. The anthropologist Jon Mitchell suggests that rather than generating 'a coherent ... theory of agency, resistance and subjectivity' that might compete with that of Bourdieu, 'de Certeau sees action – and particularly the action of everyday resistance – as relatively autonomous from socially-derived subjectivity, and rooted in a much more fundamental human nature ... agency and the capacity to resist seem to originate in the irreducible essence of the person' (2007: 91).

Thus Bourdieu and de Certeau offer different answers to the question of the nature of practices. Bourdieu rejects the binary of resistance and submission through a notion of relationality, as emphasised in his (1987: 184) point that 'Resistance can be alienating and submission can be liberating' and submission is not a conscious choice, but 'is lodged deep in the socialized body' (cited by Wacquant in Bourdieu and Wacquant 1992: 24). In contrast de Certeau's approach depends on a problematic binary (see also Lee and Ingold 2006) in which the strategies of the powerful and the tactics of the weak are set against each other. Moreover, while the idea that human resistance is not simply an internalisation of the habitus is appealing, locating 'agency and the capacity to resist ... in the irreducible essence of the person' (Mitchell 2007, Napolitano and Pratten 2007: 6) does not provide a full explanation either. By viewing the arguments of de Certeau and Bourdieu comparatively, it emerges that in common they have become part of a debate over whether we should characterise practices as resistant or normative. An alternative is to consider practice as a more open analytical concept that stands for human actions that may have multiple potentials. Thus seeing practices as possibly resulting in forms of everyday innovation, self-conscious resistance or as maintaining a sense of stability. In the next section I consider some of these issues in relation to more recent developments in practice theory.

THEORIES OF PRACTICE AND THE SOCIOLOGY OF CONSUMPTION

Reviewing practice theory at the beginning of the twenty-first century, the philosopher Schatzki established a set of commonalities between practice approaches. Most theorists of practice, he writes, 'conceive of them minimally, as arrays of activity' and although he points out that there are variations in how different theorists have defined these, he identifies a series of themes which can be set out as: practice as activity, practice as tacit ways of knowing, practice as human/non-human and practice as embodied. From this perspective, practices are not just individual or dislocated from a bigger context, but fundamental to understanding the society they are part of. Central to this understanding, Schatzki tells us, is 'the notion of a field of practice'. This refers to 'the total nexus of interconnected human practices' (Schatzki 2001: 2), the components of which include 'knowledge, meaning, human activity, science, power, language, social institutions, and historical transformation' (Schatzki 2001: 2). Thus, by putting practice at the centre of the analysis, practice theorists seek to comprehend the relationship between the detail of everyday activities (the enacting of practices) and a wider society.

In recent years practice theory, as developed by Schatzki (1996, 2001), has become increasingly popular in sociological approaches to consumption and everyday life. The sociologist Alan Warde's (2005) discussion of how practice theory might be applied to the sociology of consumption has been highly influential in this. For Warde, consumption – understood as 'a process whereby agents engage in appropriation and appreciation' (2005: 137) – is not a practice but 'a moment in almost every practice' (2005: 137). He suggests that appropriation 'occurs within practices' and 'Practices, rather than individual desires create wants' (2005: 137). Warde's rendering of practice theory draws from Schatzki's notion of practice as both 'entity' and 'performance' (2005: 133–4) thus leading him to argue that 'At any given point in time a practice has a set of established understandings, procedures and objectives' (2005: 140) and to stress the role of convention in the way people engage in practices (2005: 140). Because contemporary practice theorists place practices at the centre of their analysis, they inevitably situate the individual practitioner in a way that is subordinate to the practice itself. Following Schatzki, for practice theorists, individuals are not 'the source of meaning and normativity', rather 'practices are the source and carriers of meaning, language and normativity' (2001: 12). Yet, as Warde acknowledges, a practice approach can also accommodate change in that practices are performed differently by different people, which means that 'practices also contain the seeds of constant change. They are dynamic by virtue of their own internal logic of operation, as people in myriad situations adapt, improvise and experiment' (2005: 141). Warde's ideas have been taken up across a number of areas of consumption (see Halkier et al. 2011 for a good review of the application of practice theory in consumer research). This includes their engagement precisely in the analysis of kitchen practices (e.g. Martens 2012) and laundry practices (Gram-Hanssen 2008), which are discussed in Chapters 4 and 5 respectively, as well as by scholars studying media practices (e.g. Bräuchler and Postill 2010), which in Chapters 7 and 8 are brought to the fore in analysing how digital media are implicated in activism. These existing studies, as well as the approach itself, importantly show how approaching everyday life through practices offers the researcher a route through which to enter the complexity that everyday life is.

Yet, the study of practices, when undertaken ethnographically, cannot but also be the study of individuals as they are engaged in practices (see also Pink 2004). Indeed, the ethnographic approach I outline in Chapter 3 foregrounds the experiential and the individual elements of the performance of practices. As I noted at the beginning of this chapter, here theoretical approaches are engaged not simply to shape the analysis of ethnographic findings, but to respond to the understandings that emerge from ethnographic research. Ethnographic research thus brings into question the emphasis on practices as an analytical unit, and invites us to ask further questions, such as how does the individual performance of practice intersect with, for instance, biography, memory, discourse, sensory experience, materiality, sociality or the weather? The implication is that an analytical focus on practices might be enhanced through a focus that also involves understanding individuals, and moreover taking individual performance and experience as an analytical unit that can lead to understandings of processes of change. As recent anthropological research demonstrates, attention to the detail of how individuals learn, engage in, experience and know through practices enables us to better understand the implications of the specificities of the performance of practice for wider social issues. For instance, the anthropologist Trevor Marchand, discussing his ethnographic apprenticeship in carpentry, writes how '[a]t every turn in the process, there lies the possibility of misinterpretation, or new interpretation, and the carrying forward of ideas and practices in novel directions. Making things is therefore making knowledge'. As Marchand argues, 'By carefully studying these micro-processes, we stand a better chance of describing the mechanics of social and cultural change' (2010: S118). I discuss the implications of anthropological approaches further in the second part of this chapter. My argument here is that an ethnographic focus on individual performances shows how and why individuals modify and re-create practices as they perform them.

A focus on the individual thus invites ways to understand practices as producing both stability and change. While the ways individuals engage in collective practices may produce normative behaviours and sustain standards, it is just as possible that they will be innovative and might chip away at established norms. Innovative twists or acts of resistance are not necessarily internal to the practice itself, but may be related to biographical, discursive, activist and other currents that converge in how individuals perform particular practices. Likewise however, it should not be assumed that just because a practice sustains normative values, its capacity to do so is simply internal to the practice itself. Rather, the (perhaps unlikely) event that innovation will not emerge from practice itself needs to be explained by situating practice. In Chapter 4, through a comparison of the detail of how two individuals perform the practices of washing up and kitchen cleaning, I demonstrate how biography, memory and sociality, along with the material and sensory environment of the kitchen, are implicated in the performance of practices. Yet, as I show, acknowledgement of the importance of the individual is not enough to comprehend what it is that configures a practice in a particular form. Rather, both individuals and practices need to be understood as part of wider configurations, which in turn explain how practices are performed and thus constituted.

GOING BEYOND PRACTICE

The above discussion reveals how practice theory takes us some way to explaining why certain practices are maintained, how norms might be sustained and how innovation is achieved through the performance of practices. Yet, as Barry Barnes points out, 'no "theory of practice" can be a sufficient basis for an understanding of human behaviour, or even that part of it which is orderly and routine' (2001: 18). In short, we need to account for how practices intersect with other processes and things.

The relationship between body, mind and the material and sensory environment is increasingly central to contemporary scholarship (see, for example, Ingold 2000, Howes 2005b, Pink 2009a). Indeed understandings of embodiment and materiality are part of a practice approach which considers that 'the social is a field of embodied, materially interwoven practices centrally organized around shared practice understanding' (Schatzki 2001: 3), and part of 'the total nexus of interconnected human practices' (Schatzki 2001: 2). Some scholars who work with practice theory have already begun to build on Schatzki's practice approach to account further for materiality, the senses and the environment. For example, Shove et al. contend that practice theory (e.g. Schatzki 1996, Reckwitz 2002) accounts insufficiently for the role of 'things' – and where they are acknowledged (e.g. by Warde 2005), there is 'a somewhat limited treatment of things as passive means of accomplishing practices, not as active co-constitutive elements of the practice itself' (Shove et al. 2007: 13). Shove et al. therefore propose combining practice theory with Bruno Latour's (1992) ideas to explore the roles of non-human actors – 'materials, tools and technologies …
in the making, reproduction and transformation of practices' (2007: 14) in domestic contexts. Likewise, focusing on the senses and space, the geographer Kirsten Simonsen, who also roots her argument in

Schatzki's practice approach, seeks to 'give meaning to unnoticed and apparently insignificant activities of everyday life' (2007: 168) by calling for a consideration of 'the sensuous character of practice' and 'the spatialities involved in that character' (2007: 169). These ways of attending to practices in relation to other elements of the environment – materiality, technology, the senses – begin to raise questions about how we understand embodied practices in relation to the wider ecologies they are part of; where environments are not just social, material and technological, but multisensory, charged with energy, emotion, shifting with the weather, and contingent on the activity of non-human organisms too.

The implication is that to situate practices we need a concept that enables us to comprehend how practices are part of an environment and how therefore elements of our lives such as energy, sunlight, warmth, the feel of newly laundered sheets, the taste of local produce or the viewing of a YouTube video are interrelated with our everyday actions. As I outlined above a practice approach can be used to help explain why some human activities appear normative and are sustained and also how practices are transformed as they are performed. Yet this approach is less able to account for the contingency and fluidity that can also characterise everyday life, or the irregularity, messiness and inconsistency that ethnographers often encounter. Nor does it fully account for the multiple other processes with which practices might become interwoven. In the remainder of this chapter, I examine how a theory of place can support an understanding of practice as part of such wider ecologies.

BEYOND THE QUALITIES OF PLACE: ABSTRACTIONS AND LOCALITIES

As for theories of practice discussed above, there is no single commonly applied theory of place; moreover geographers point to the diversity in how notions of space and place have been used, resulting in their being 'relatively diffuse, ill-defined and inchoate concepts' (Hubbard et al. 2004: 6). In this book I follow a definition of place as an abstract concept understood as distinct from the notion of locality. This is intended as a universal definition of place, which stands as a framework for understanding how different processes and things combine to create the world as it is experienced. Yet to counter the problems that anthropologists have indentified, in that a universal approach to place may override local people's own conceptualisations of place (e.g. see Hirsch 1995), this approach is also used alongside one that is centred more closely on human subjects, to account for local people's understandings of place – what might be thought of as a 'sense of place' – and the ways in which this is created – the notion of 'place-making'. Places, as understood here, as an abstract concept, therefore do not necessarily exhibit particular *qualities* or have predetermined effects in the world. In this sense, like practices, places are entities that are constantly changing. Yet, because they are experienced, both by ethnographers and by research partici-pants, they are always subjectively defined. This approach is to be distin-guished from that in which an empirically defined type of place has specified qualities, as developed in Marc Augé's distinction between places and non-places. Augé refers to, on the one hand, 'empirical non-places' which are 'spaces of circulation, consumption and communica-tion'. These he contrasts with 'anthropological place[s]' – a 'space in which inscription of the social bond (for example, places where strict rules of residence are imposed on everyone) or collective history (for example, places of worship) can be seen' (Augé 2008: viii). He therefore invites us to use 'place' to describe actual empirical material realities (e.g. villages, towns, neighbourhoods, etc.), which have particular *qualities*. Rather differently my concern is with how an abstract notion of place that seeks to understand the multiple material, sensory, political and social processes that constitute the environment can enable us to understand how people create their 'sense of place' and the role of practice in this.

In what follows I discuss a theory of place that enables understandings of the empirical realities of actual experienced environments, and the practices that form a part of these. In doing so I draw from three think-ers on place: the philosopher Edward Casey (e.g. 1996), the geographer Doreen Massey (e.g. 2005) and the anthropologist Tim Ingold (e.g. 2008). Even a superficial reading of the works of these three scholars reveals their quite different understandings of the relationship between place and space. Yet discussing their ideas *in relation* to (rather than instead of) each other is a useful exercise because it brings to the fore different routes to knowing about the politics and phenomenology of place.

Following the phenomenology of Merleau-Ponty, Casey has put human perception at the centre of the analysis of place, arguing that it is primary in our capacity to know place by being 'in a place' (1996: 18). For Casey, thus, space and time 'arise from the experience of place itself' (1996: 36). His emphasis on the importance of human perception for understanding place is crucial, yet as Massey points out, Casey's approach is limited by a focus on the local, thus challenging the way he gives priority to place itself. Massey's conceptualisation of place in con-trast, is interdependent with her notion of space. She argues that space is not abstract or mappable, and not subordinate to place (see 2005: 130, 183). Rather, she sees space as 'a simultaneity of stories-so-far' and suggests that 'places are collections of those stories, articulations of the wider power-geometries of space' (2005: 130), as such place is 'a constellation of processes' (2005: 141). This understanding situates place in the context of a wider politics of space, which reminds us that there is agency beyond place. There is, however, a common theme in the renderings of place proposed by these two scholars. Casey understands place as a constantly changing 'event', with what he calls a 'gathering power' – a capacity to accumulate diverse things in its 'midst' (1996: 24). Resonating with this to some extent, Massey suggests place is a form of 'event' – places are '*spatio-temporal* events' (2005: 130, original italics), with a quality of 'throwntogetherness' (2005: 140) of things. As in Casey's idea of the gathering of place, such things might be human, material, intangible. Thus, while differing in their formulations of the relationship between place and space, Casey and Massey both seek to understand 'place' in terms of how things come together, stay together, or reconstitute in other constellations. Their rather different approaches to answering this question raise different, although complementary questions about place. As Massey's argument shows, Casey's rendering of place is limited by the assumption that place is prior to whatever is beyond it; thus meaning it does not explain how power relations beyond place are implicated in the processes that the 'things' that are 'in' places are engaged/involved in. Massey's work in contrast, begs further thought on the question of how the detail of local activities, sensory perception and human embodied experience are implicated in the constitution of place.

Ingold's (2007, 2008) understanding of place offers us a way to consider human perception and the idea of place as unbounded within the same framework is rooted in the phenomenology of the philosopher Maurice Merleau-Ponty and of the ecological psychologist James Gibson. Following this line of thinking, perception in movement is primary to the way we experience and make meaning in our environments. For Ingold the environment is not simply something we act in or on, but something people, as organisms, are *part of* (see Ingold 2000). Ingold proposes further that 'The environment ... comprises not the surroundings of the organism but a zone of entanglement' (2008: 1797). Thus places are not bounded zones that we live or engage in practices *in* but they are actually produced through movement. We might think not only of human movement but also of that of all types of things. As such the constantly changing constellations of things that we call places are constituted through the movement of these very things, and their subsequent entanglements. These are not movements that we necessarily always observe with the eye or feel underfoot. For instance, if we think of the kitchen as a place, some movements are obvious, such as the arrival of a new fridge or installation of a skylight in the kitchen roof. Others, like the flow of gas or electricity to the oven, might be more taken for granted. When looking out of the window, geological movements, for instance, of what Massey calls 'giant rocks' (2005: 130) might go unnoticed. However, these movements are essential to understanding how place is made because, following Ingold, locality itself does not make place. Rather, as he puts it: 'there would be no places were it not for the comings and goings of human beings and other organisms to and from them, from and to places elsewhere' (2008: 1808). Another way of thinking about this is to see places as 'occur[ing] along the lifepaths of beings' as part of a 'meshwork of paths' (2008: 1808). Thus, Ingold's (2008) work allows us to both appreciate the idea of place as unbounded and open, as does Massey's (2005), albeit from a different perspective, and to understand human perception and movement as central to the process of place (see also Casey 1996).

This understanding of place therefore has practical implications for comprehending the research sites discussed in the following chapters. To work with it requires considering the idea of place as a theoretical and abstract notion rather than as an actual bounded physical location. When analysing practices associated with a context such as the kitchen, a neighbourhood, a town or the Internet, it is all too easy to conflate a theoretical reference with a commonsense assumption. Therefore, for instance, one might confuse a kitchen as a theoretical place with a lay notion of the kitchen as a place – a room – that one *goes into*, is bounded architecturally and is where certain objects and activities are confined. Indeed this seems a particularly 'natural' association to make when referring to English homes where kitchen practices (a term which has been coined mainly in the work of Lydia Martens and Sue Scott [e.g. 2004]) and architectural kitchen designs/conventions tend to coincide. However, the relationship between architectural design and actual practice is not necessarily straightforward and should not be treated as given, and thus we should make no assumption about the prior definitions of localities before they are constituted as places. In Chapter 4 I examine this point in relation to actual kitchens, and in Chapter 6 I show how likewise in the case of a community garden it is not the fence around the garden that contains the essence of what it is, but rather the movements of things through those boundaries, in, around and outside it. Indeed in Chapter 8 I argue that once the notion of place as a physical locality is relinquished, it can equally be used to analyse mediated contexts.

Such a conceptualisaiton thus offers a way of understanding practices as part of place. The geographer Tim Cresswell, drawing on Massey's definition of place, has proposed: 'To think of place as an intersection – a particular configuration of happenings – is to think of place in a constant sense of becoming through practice and practical knowledge. Place is both the context for practice – we act according to more or less stable schemes of perception – and a product of practice – something that only makes sense as it is lived' (2003: 26). The notion of a place-event therefore provides a way in which to *situate* practices of everyday life and activism, and therefore to understand the renewal or transformation of kitchens, gardens or towns. This is because as I show in Chapter 4, kitchen practices do not take place *in prior constituted kitchens*. Likewise in Chapter 6 I demonstrate that gardening is not done in a locality that is a garden independently of the practice of gardening. Rather kitchen and garden practices are co-constitutive of the event of kitchens or gardens as places in that they are part of constellations of diverse (but not necessarily unrelated) things and processes in movement. In the same way as I outline in Chapter 7, it is the practices associated with slow living that contribute to the constitution of slow towns.

UNDERSTANDINGS OF PRACTICE AND PLACE THROUGH MOVEMENT

Departures from ideas of place as locality, bounded or enclosed (Massey 2005, Ingold 2008) invite an understanding of domestic, public and mediated places and selves, knowing, memories and imaginings as constituted through 'entanglements' that involve ongoing practices. Thus, following the idea of place as a theoretical abstraction rather than as referring to *actual* material localities as units for scholarly analysis (see also Pink 2009a) I understand place as a shifting intensity or a constellation of things (or in Massey's [2005] terms, processes), of which practices are a part.

Above, I have stressed the idea that movement is integral to the constitution of place. Practices too, conceptualised as activities, involve movement. Therefore how can we conceptualise the relationship between place, practice and movement? One way to approach this is through an interrogation of movement. Reflecting on mobility and movement, Cresswell stresses the relationship between representation and practice. He suggests there are: 'three aspects of mobility: the fact of physical movement – getting from one place to another; the representations of movement that give it shared meaning; and, finally, the experienced and embodied practice of movement. In practice these elements of mobility are unlikely to be easy to untangle. They are bound up with one another' (2010: 20). In this sense, and following Ingold's (2007, 2008) emphasis on the role of movement in the constitution of place, we can understand practice as part of the process through which place is constituted, while following Cresswell to note that representations also participate in ecologies of place.

Therefore, practices, material agencies, skills and ways of knowing don't happen *in* places that their practitioners go to in order to perform them. Rather they are constituents of places. Practices happen in movement, and their performance and the knowing that this entails are inextricable from place. But the places of practices are themselves constituted through movement. They are unbounded and do not frame practices though a field of fixed logic. Rather, as Cresswell suggests, 'Place provides a template for practice – an unstable stage for performance. Thinking of place as performed and practiced can help us think of place in radically open and non-essentialized ways where place is constantly struggled over and reimagined in practical ways' (2003: 25). As such place can also be seen as the coming together of the components through which ways of reproducing conventions or creating innovations are constituted in everyday life and where the interweaving of the representations, and embodied practices, that thought-out activism entails is played out. Therefore, an understanding of place as open is crucial for an understanding of the openness and potentialities of practice that I have proposed above.

The detail of human practice needs to be situated within a constantly changing constellation of diverse 'things' (meaning: agencies, discourses, representations, materialities, persons, sensory and affective qualities, memories, texts and more). The practices of everyday life cannot be lived or understood in isolation from individual practitioners in movement, from representations, or from the event (Massey 2005) or 'occurrence' (Ingold 2008) of place with which they are inevitably entangled.

CONCLUSION: THINKING THROUGH THE PRACTICES AND PLACES OF EVERYDAY LIFE

Everyday life is not to be seen as something that is static, but a dynamic and changing site. Theories of practice and place support this understanding and offer us routes to research the processes of consumption, innovation and activism through which everyday transformations become 'visible', and which may or may not lead us to a sustainable future.

It should by now be clear that practices of any kind must be understood as part of wider environments and activities. As I have shown above, theorists of practice and their critics have sought to find ways of locating practices within some wider matrix. This has involved ideas about fields of practice, about human–material relations and excursions into spatial theory. A theory of place that focuses on movement and knowing and that acknowledges the diversity of 'things' and processes that converge in what Massey (2005: 141) calls the 'event of place' allows us to situate the practices of everyday life in such a way that recognises their interwoveness with and contingency on other processes, materialities and representations. Such a framework does not pin down practices into static contexts, but allows them the dynamism of operating within constantly changing constellations or ecologies. This allows both the lived reality of practice and the event of place to be understood as contingent and as mutually interdependent.

Thus the question of what comes first – practices or places – is rendered obsolete. Neither precedes the other. Both are theoretical constructs that have been developed to understand things that are *already happening*. They both offer an abstract route to comprehending complex processes. There is no 'real' or correct empirical starting point, rather only starting points for scholarly knowing. One of the tasks of this book is also to establish the intersections between these theories as starting points for understanding the environments and activities of everyday life and activism in a series of different contexts. In Chapter 3, I explore how we might go about seeking such understandings.

3

RESEARCHING PRACTICES, PLACES AND REPRESENTATIONS: METHODOLOGIES AND METHODS

The everyday is where we live our lives. It is subsequently a site from which research, activism and intervention emerge and are increasingly combined in new ways as engaged scholars become implicated in projects that seek to bring about changes. Yet we cannot directly capture its constant flow. It both prevails on us and slips through our fingers. This methodological problem is equally insistent regardless of the disciplinary origins of the researcher or research topic, yet scholars who root their epistemologies in, for instance, sociology, geography, cultural studies or anthropology deal with it in different ways. Very broadly this might involve choices between treating the everyday as data, as representation or as a route to knowing. Yet there is emerging a new consciousness about the question of how to research everyday life and activism across academic disciplines, which raises common concerns. In this chapter I develop a critical discussion of the issues and strategies surrounding the question of how we might approach and go about researching practices and places. In doing so I also introduce into the discussion the question of representations.

INTERDISCIPLINARY METHODOLOGICAL CONCERNS

As the study of practice, places and representations is an interdisciplinary field, the epistemological commitments that inform the way they are researched by different scholars tend to be rooted in their own disciplinary trajectories. Yet across disciplinary boundaries there is emerging a set of common concerns that invite us to reflect on questions relating to the contexts and the methods we use for researching everyday life and activism. These include sensory aesthetics, the use of media, collaborative methods, the reflexivity of being *in* the everyday, and accounting for the 'flow' of everyday life. I first explore these issues and highlight their implications for the following discussions of how we might research the places, practices and representations of everyday life and activism developed in the remainder of the chapter.

A constant dilemma for the scholar of everyday life is the question of how she or he might both live it and study it. For instance, Gardiner emphasises how: 'we cannot simply "go to" the everyday; we are "always-already" immersed in it' (2009: 385) and Sheringham discusses the methodology of 'the project' which he suggests '"allows for" everydayness by suspending abstract definition and creating a breathing space, a gap or hiatus that enables the *quotidien* to be apprehended as a medium in which we are immersed rather than as a category to be analyzed' (2006: 390, original italics). For the activist scholar this is likewise a concern, but in a more explicit way, in that she or he is part of, and an active agent in the process she or he is studying. To deal with this question requires the recognition that researchers are in some way always part of the lives and worlds they are researching. We are engaged with research participants or with representations in ways that are practical, creative, imaginative and empathetic, and these engagements form part of research practice. This however is not a new problem; the issue that as researchers we are part of the lives and worlds (albeit temporarily in some cases) of research participants has long since been a concern for anthropologists, and forms a fundamental part of contemporary reflexive ethnographic practice. Indeed the development of a reflexive approach that attends to the process of knowledge production, its intersubjectivity and the power relations that are embedded in it has been increasingly incorporated in ethnographic practice since the emergence of Clifford and Marcus's seminal volume on *Writing Culture* (1986) in the 1980s. Such an approach enables researchers working with either people whose lives are very different from their own, or conversely with people with whom they share much in common, to comprehend an everyday world of which they are already or have, through the research process, become a part. The anthropological ethnographer maintains a high level of self-consciousness concerning the processes and sensory, embodied and affective experiences and gendered relationships through which she or he comes to know about other people's everyday lives – whether or not this involves doing research through participant observation or through contemporary innovative methods. A broad literature emerged around these questions and research practices in anthropology and sociology during the 1990s (e.g. Bell et al. 1993, Kulick and Wilson 1995, Coffey 1999) and continues to interrogate questions around ethnographic knowing in more recent work (e.g. Harris 2007, Halstead et al. 2008). Such a reflexive approach is integral to the visual and sensory methodologies (Pink 2007a, 2009a) that inform the research discussed in the following chapters.

A turn to the reflexive and participatory approaches of anthropological ethnography is thus particularly useful in the task of understanding everyday life and moreover responds to critical concerns about other methodologies in everyday life studies. For example, Gardiner points to the inadequacies of empirical sociological approaches to everyday life rooted in 'ethnomethodology, symbolic interactionism, the phenomenology of Alfred Schütz and Berger and Luckman, and Erving Goffman's "dramaturgology"' (2000: 4) for this task. These, he complains, 'tend to reinforce, rather than subvert, the pervasive dichotomy between specialized and non-specialized knowledges' (2000: 5) and 'none of them really seek to abandon the pretence to objectivity, scholarly detachment and non-partisanship that has served to legitimate the social sciences for the last 150 years' (2000: 5). The reflexive approach outlined above conversely acknowledges the impossibility of objectivity. It treats research knowledge as co-produced ways of knowing rather than objective 'data' and research as an inevitably collaborative process, and thus offers a route to knowing about everyday life that is coherent with the calls emerging from within the work of theorists of everyday life. It also stands for an approach to 'researching with' rather than simply about people, and in this sense is also compatible with participatory, activist or intervention research where participants might become co-producers or users of research knowledge.

In Chapter 2, I suggested that researchers of practices and places are concerned with the study of people and things in movement. This raises the question of how to research moving subjects in a world in movement. In existing literature the understanding that we are at the same time researching and part of the continuous and unstoppable flow of everyday life creates a methodological dilemma, which applies alike to the theorist and the ethnographer of the everyday. For Highmore the problem for the theorist lies in this: 'If, for example, the everyday is seen as a "flow", then any attempt to arrest it, to apprehend it, to scrutinize it, will be problematic' (2002: 21). Another approach is encapsulated through non-representational theory as conceptualised by the geographer Nigel Thrift. Non-representational theory, Thrift tells us, 'tries to capture the "onflow", as Ralph Pred (2005) calls it, of everyday life' (2008: 5). For the ethnographer, if we locate knowing and the moment of meaning making at the constantly shifting intersections between practice and other constituents of the event of place, likewise it appears difficult to extract and crystallise knowledge from this process. Indeed the researcher is confronted with a moving subject in several senses of the terms that she or he is seeking to understand: persons and things that are in movement; ways of knowing that are subject to change; and representations that also move and whose meanings are contingent on the constantly shifting configurations through which they are interpreted. It is therefore by understanding these persons and things as, along with the researcher, part of the event of place, that we might understand how everyday life can be researched and represented – in movement.

Certain research methods are compatible with such an understanding, based on the principle that to research a moving research subject one should literally do research in movement – through an embodied and sensory engagement with the practices and places of those people and things we are doing research with. In this context mobile methodologies, often using visual methods and media, are becoming increasingly popular across disciplines. The ethnographies discussed in Chapters 4–6 are based on this principle and below I discuss how the use of video in the (re)enactment of practices and in place-making walking tours can facilitate an approach that enables ethnographers to do research in movement and maintain a sense of that movement when (re)reviewing research materials. However, as I stressed in Chapter 2, it is not just people who move, but also things, and the movement of non–humans is also crucial to the constitution of place. In Chapter 5, I develop an approach that follows the flows of domestic material culture through the home and in Chapter 6, I emphasise the importance of tracing the routes through which plants and garden furniture arrived in a community garden. An approach that follows the flows of people and things does not need to seek to 'capture' or 'arrest' the flow of everyday life, but to follow it, and to gain a *sense* of it.

This approach also has implications for how we understand representations as part of everyday life and activism, as well as for the ways in which researchers might understand everyday life through its representations. It means conceiving of representations not as stopping points or crystallisations that become fixed in a permanent location or as holding fixed and internal meanings. Rather, I argue that representations should be understood as being produced and comprehended in and through movement and in ways that are shifting and contingent. Representations (e.g. written texts, images, performances, video recordings, art works and more) hold together a range of characters, images or sounds on pages or in digital compositions. These might be materially or digitally finished and as such fixed in their form (although in the case of digital representations this is often not the case). Yet like the persons and material culture discussed above they are not static but are embedded in fields of shifting relations and meanings. Scholarly representations are likewise made and consumed in movement, through practice and in particular environments. They become involved in the further making of meanings as their trajectories become entangled with ours and with those of others. This paragraph, for instance, has been produced through my own embodied practice, writing at a computer, it will be printed and turned into electronic copy, be given meaning by its readers and perhaps cited by other authors. Thus it becomes possible to comprehend the flow of everyday life and the production and meaning making of representations of everyday life as part of the same process. We are always in movement and constantly making representations. Images, texts and other representations need not be understood simply as attempts to hold up and scrutinise the flow of everyday life. They are, following the theoretical arguments outlined in Chapter 2, rather, part of and inseparable from the process through which we move as we live. Therefore the goal of the scholar of everyday life or activism is not to find ways to cut across the places and practices where everyday life and activism are played out and examine the flat surface that is left or to take representations as finished texts to analyse in terms of their content. Rather, she or he should find her or his way through its unevenness, following those whose lives, actions and things she or he seeks to understand. It is indeed by following people, things, representations and narratives that we encounter the very trails that are important and arrive at the intersections where meanings and changes are made.

In Chapter 1, I outlined how across the social sciences and humanities there is an increasing focus on the senses and aesthetics. This emphasis has raised new questions about and approaches to how we might research practices, places and representations in different disciplinary traditions and research practices including ethnography and textual analysis. A sensory ethnography (Pink 2009a) attends to the multisensoriality of the ways in which ethnographers and research participants experience their lives and worlds, and to the tacit and unspoken as well as verbal actions and categories they use to classify and represent these to others. It is as such concerned with how we come to know in practice, in movement and in ways that are nonverbal. Yet simultaneously a multisensory approach recognises the role and practice of representation in the ways in which research participants and researchers communicate about and make experiences explicit to others. The multisensory approach to ethnography, as developed in the research and analysis discussed in Chapters 4–8, also depends on a theory of place, as developed in Chapter 2. It situates both the participants in the research and the ethnographer her or himself as emplaced and, simultaneously through their practices (of everyday life and research), constituents and constitutive of places (see Pink 2009a for a detailed development of this).

The senses have also been placed on the agenda of everyday life studies, specifically in terms of a concern with the question of textual analysis and by Highmore with reference to the potential of an 'archive of everyday life'. Cultural studies, Highmore points out, is 'massively underdeveloped in relation to the aural, the olfactory and the haptic' while having 'developed sophisticated ways of attending to the *semiotic material* of the visual and verbal' (Highmore 2002: 26, my italics), thus suggesting the possibility of 'reading' the 'haptical' in photographic images (Highmore 2002: 26). However, while it is possible that the analysis of photographs can imply or invoke certain haptic experiences, semiotic readings of sensory experiences have some limits. For example, in relation to the semiotic perspective of the multimodality paradigm, Dicks et al. have argued that 'Photographs allow us to see modes that are visual: colour, shape, size, position, light' but do not reveal modes 'that operate through the other senses – of touch, smell, hearing and taste – such as bodily movement, texture, three-dimensional shape, sounds' (2006: 88). However a shift away from semiotic analysis towards analysing photographs and other representations through a theory of mutlisensoriality and place offers an alternative route to knowledge. The relationship between visual and haptic senses has already been stressed in visual anthropology (MacDougall 1998) and film theory (Marks 2000). In particular MacDougall suggests that while seeing and touching are not 'interchangeable', they 'share an experiential field', each referring 'to a more general faculty' (MacDougall 1998: 51) (see also Pink 2009a for further discussion). This enables us to conceptualise ways to analyse the visuality of photographs in terms of their capacity to evoke multisensory experience that might then be expressed or interpreted in terms of sensory categories such as the visual, touch, sound, taste or smell. Thus, rather than using a semiotic method of 'reading' representations, I take an approach to text rooted in phenomenological anthropology. This, as I show in Chapters 7 and 8 respectively, enables an understanding of digital and analogue photograph and web platform materials. I outline this approach further below through a discussion of researching representations.

Scholars are not only interested in media and representations as texts to be analysed. Rather, arts and media production practices are increasingly implicated in processes of academic and applied research and representation. This can be seen in the increasing use of visual methods and media in research practice (see Pink 2007a) in the cross-over between ethnography, intervention and activism (Pink 2007b) and in the development of links with artistic practice (e.g. Schneider and Wright 2005, 2010, Pink 2009a). The everyday life scholar Sheringham also probes this area, asking: 'Do specific genres or media have particular virtues in granting access to, or purchase on, the everyday? Or does the everyday seem to slip between the fingers, so to speak, of established genres and, by virtue of an inherent elusiveness, seem to escape the purview of, say, narrative fiction, lyric poetry, drama, film, photography, pictorial art, reportage, thriving rather on the indeterminacy offered by the transgression of generic boundaries?' (2006: 15). I suggest that the answer lies not in the question of if we can capture or encounter the everyday in such texts or art works, but rather in how artists, media producers and (activist) scholars might engage them to invoke life as it is lived in ways that are place-contingent. One route to connecting researchers and audiences to the everyday is by creating empathetic dialogue (sensory and verbal) with participants in the research. This approach is represented in the work of the French filmmaker Jean Rouch, which forms a common influence in everyday life studies and visual ethnography practice, including in the contemporary work of activist-scholars. Rouch's vision of a 'shared anthropology' (Rouch 2003 [1973]), whereby film participants and filmmakers mutually engage in the production processes, has been influential in recent (visual) ethnography ranging from visual methods to anthropological filmmaking (see Pink 2007b). Sheringham also calls on Rouch's practice as an example of approaching the everyday. He characterises *Chronique d'un ete* (1961), which Rouch made with the sociologist Edgar Morin as a film where 'The film-makers are active participants throughout, and the interactions between themselves, and with other protagonists, create a space of exchange where the *quotidian* is approached from within an individual and collective matrix rather than from the outside' (2006: 13, original italics). Such approaches and the enduring influence of Rouch continue to be represented in contemporary visual ethnography and activist-scholar ethnographic filmmaking (see Pink 2007b). They moreover inform the collaborative video touring and walking with video methods (Pink 2007a, 2009a) that produced the research discussed in Chapters 4–6 and are becoming increasingly mainstream in visual methods practice. These methods are discussed further below.

The issues concerning flow, reflexivity, the senses and media are ongoing concerns for qualitative researchers, whatever their substantive focus. In what follows I explore their implications for the more practical ways in which we might go about researching the places, practices and representations of activism, and in so doing outline the methods engaged in the projects discussed in Chapters 4–8.

ENCOUNTERING EVERYDAY PLACE

Chapters 4–8 of this book represent a methodological trajectory in my own work, which has developed through a focus on people's relationships with their environments in the context of everyday life and activist practices. This has involved developing research methods that are appropriate and as part of the environments I work in. Just as everyday life and its practices and representations might be situated as part of place, so may our practices of research and its representation and engagements with persons and things. This approach both builds on and departs from existing developments and critiques relating to place in ethnography. I first outline these points of departure before discussing methods of researching place in more detail.

During the 1990s, there was an increasing appreciation of place as a site for ethnographic research. For example, Stephen Feld and Keith Basso's volume (1996) *Senses of Place* drew together a set of beautifully detailed ethnographies to 'describe and interpret some of the ways which people encounter places, perceive them, and invest them with significance' (1996: 8). In doing so their volume invites us to attend to the senses, place and locality. Yet it tends to define places *as* localities. This was closely followed by the work of Gupta and Ferguson, which firmly debunked the assumption that cultures are fixed in places. They sought to break down what they refer to as the 'assumed isomorphism of space, place and culture' (1997: 34). They suggest instead 're-thinking difference *through* connection' (original italics), which will also enable us to see more clearly how power relations are implicated (1997: 34–5). This framework encourages ethnographers to account for flows and movement, and demonstrates the inadequacy of conceptual tools that equate place and culture. Yet it maintains an understanding of place as exhibiting certain qualities, and as an empirical reality rather than a conceptual tool. Gupta and Ferguson propose that the existing 'uncontestable observation' that 'space is made meaningful' should be politicised to ask: '[H]ow are spatial meanings established? *Who has the power to make places out of spaces?* Who contests this? What is at stake?' (1997: 40, my italics). These issues of power and contestation remain pertinent. However, as I outlined in Chapter 2, my departure from these approaches involves re-thinking how the concept of place is employed through a focus on the concept of the event of place. From this perspective (following Massey's

2005 point), while cultures are indeed not fixed in places, neither are places fixed in localities or made out of empty spaces. As I have outlined elsewhere (Pink 2009a) also requires that we acknowledge how the researcher her or himself becomes part of place, as she or he is involved in a locality, encounters the social, sensory and material elements of that environment, and her or his trajectory becomes temporarily intertwined with the people and things that also constitute that place. To follow these points through involves re-figuring the relationship between the idea of a research site and a place. It requires making a clear distinction between a locality such as the town, the garden, the breakfast held in a town hall and the place-event as a way of understanding the shifting configurations of persons, things, practices, emotions, climatic conditions and more in relation to a locality. In the latter way of thinking, places themselves do not exist independently and we cannot go off and find them and do ethnography or interviews in them. Rather, we are part of the constitution of the research-place-event as we do research: Thus leading to the making of what I have elsewhere called 'ethnographic places' (Pink, 2009a). As we shall see in Chapter 8, this point is of particular relevance when we consider places that unite online and offline contexts and the idea of doing ethnography in virtual places. Therefore, the research contexts I consider in the following chapters are not simply localities, but rather, the intensities of everyday social relationships, materialities, sensory experiences, practices, representations, discourses and more – following Massey they are 'spatio-temporal events' (2005: 130). Therefore, as researchers of and in place-events, our task is to understand not what happens *in* homes, neighbourhoods, towns or web platforms as if they were bounded units across whose borders we can cross when we enter them. But rather, we seek to understand how intensities of place occur through the coming together of localities, materialities, socialities and other constituents. In Chapter 2, I stressed how the place-event has been conceptualised as constantly shifting – in movement. Moreover, it is not just the research subject(s)/particpants and the materialities and representations that are part of their lives that move, but researchers too. When as researchers we move in/through an environment, we are moving as Ingold's (e.g. 2010a) work suggests as *part of* that environment, and anything we do contributes to its constitution.

Thus the methods used to produce the research discussed in the following chapters specifically addressed environments in movement. It is an everyday reality that people are constantly moving around in their homes. So too are the material objects that are part of the home. The research method of purposely walking around and exploring their homes with research participants can enable us to both recognise how the home is experienced in movement and to chart the movement of things in the home. Elsewhere I have written extensively about the domestic video tour (e.g. Pink 2004, 2006, 2007a). This involved my video recording the research participants while they led me around their homes. The domestic practices discussed in Chapter 4 were preceded by a video tour focused on the ways in which participants cared for and cleaned their homes, their home decoration and what the material and sensory culture of their homes meant to them. The research discussed in Chapter 5 had a similar focus but specifically explored the home in terms of 'laundry flows'. By moving *through* the home with the participant I did not reconstruct the actual experience of everyday life in the home, yet I encountered the sensoriality of home, the surfaces underfoot, the smells and the textures. The material context of the home invoked commentaries from participants about their memories, experiences, values and practices and enabled us to trace the routes that the material culture of laundry took through the home. The idea of walking around a neighbourhood, city or other environment as a way of defining it, experiencing it or representing it to others is also well established and has been associated with the idea of researching place. Pierre Mayol, as part of de Certeau's project of the practice of everyday life, conceptualised the neighbourhood as a unit of analysis that could be defined in terms of a walk, writing: 'The neighborhood appears as a domain in which the space-time relationship is the most favorable for a dweller who moves from place to place *on foot, starting from his or her home*', in short 'it is the result of a *walk*' (de Certeau et al. 1998: 10, original italics). The discussion in Chapter 6 draws on a series of video and photographic walking tours (e.g. see Pink 2009a) of a community garden, along with interviews and committee meetings. Each method allowed differential access to understanding the different practices of talking about, gardening in and the flows that constituted the garden. Likewise the fieldwork discussed in Chapter 7 involved mobile engagements with the practices of slow city activists in different environments, with or without my camera and often as a form of participant engagement with their activities at public festive events. There, a number of local activities and trajectories are analysed and we see that by following people, material culture, narratives and representations, a notion of how local entanglements are built up can be composed. Here, by combining explicitly mobile methods with other forms of being there, and ethnographic hanging around, I was able to engage with the experiential ways of being in towns and involvement in their events, and as such with the multisensory experience of place. Finally, doing research online, as I show in Chapter 8, involves another way of researching place. As I discuss in the final section of this chapter, through a reflection on how we might re-think research with representations, the analysis of web pages and platforms should go beyond their treatment as representations to generate an understanding of the relationship between online and material contexts in terms of a multi-sensory and embodied experience. Theoretically such a series of inter-woven things, experiences and trajectories is a place that we move through just as much as a home or a garden. Researching place thus involves moving through environments which might be material, sensory, digital and mediated.

RESEARCHING PRACTICES/IN PRACTICE

In correspondence with the increasing interest in practice among scholars across the social sciences, there is a growing need for methods for researching practices. Often such research seeks to understand elements of everyday life activities that are not necessarily immediately visible or often verbalised. This might be because they involve practices that are seldom done in public or social contexts, such as housework and home decoration (Pink 2004). Or it may be because they are concerned with things people just do – multisensory embodied practices – rather than things they normally discuss verbally in any explicit or reflexive way. These include the domestic practices discussed in Chapters 4 and 5, as well as activities such as gardening, discussed in Chapter 6, and explicitly activist practices, as outlined in Chapters 7 and 8. The research about practices discussed in this book is drawn from a combination of interviews about practices and people's experiences of them, and the engaged study of practices as they are performed – *in practice*. As I have argued in Chapter 2, the performance of practice is a key site for understanding processes of change. Therefore, methodologically, it is important to seek routes to accessing practices as they are performed. The ways in which this can be achieved are contingent, however, on other elements of the research environment, most notably in the case of whether one is doing research in the privacy of the domestic home or in a public context.

Sociologists of consumption influenced by the practice turn in scholarship have used qualitative methods to examine domestic practices. I discuss some of this work in Chapters 4 and 5. Their focus has tended to be on analysing the reported rather than performative elements of everyday life. The use of verbal reporting by research participants in the format of the interview is the most established and prevalent sociological research method. It provides a valuable route to knowledge about how people describe their activities and values, and how they feel about their homes and the practices they engage in at home. It allows focus on individual variation or on collective patterning. Interviews have been appropriately lauded for their ability to produce conversational, emotional and empathetic research encounters, and to give voice to those who are not normally heard. They can show us how people represent verbally and classify their sensory experiences of specific environments, localities, performances and practices (see Pink 2009a), and in this sense offer a useful way of understanding the representational layers of everyday life. Yet interviews are also limited in the routes to knowing about other people's experiences that they can offer in terms of providing understandings of how sensory environments and the performance of practice are experienced and the moments of meaning making. Some sociologists of practice have begun to develop new ways of accounting for practice as performed. One example is the work of Lydia Martens and Sue Scott, who have used CCTV and other video recording methods to research kitchen practices (Martens and Scott 2004, Martens 2012). Anthropologists of the home, on the other hand, have long since gone beyond the interview. As Danny Miller has pointed out, 'ethnographic encounters' within the contexts of domestic homes require anthropologists to engage in research that 'seems intrusive' because the anthropologists being there within the home is needed. This he justifies by making the very important point that 'we need to understand through empathy, the diverse ways in which this intimate relationship [between people and their homes] is being developed as the foundation to so many people's lives' (2001: 1). Research findings that are based solely on participants' verbally *reported* practices cannot facilitate an analysis of their actual practices and of how these are performed, experienced and involve specific ways of knowing *in practice*. Therefore to examine the phenomenology of everyday life that is surely fundamental to understanding how sustainable everyday life practices in the home are actually *known* and how activist practices are experienced and can be communicated about, it requires engaged methods that enable researchers to comprehend the detail of practice, the biographical and collective memories and meanings that it invokes, the non-verbalised ways of knowing that it entails. Building on the discussion in the previous section, here practices are seen as happening as part of the flow and movement of everyday life. Like persons and things, practices are never static. They do not stand still in time and are subject to constant innovation and revision as they are performed. Many practices can be thought of as involving practitioners making a series of skilled movements that in combination lead to the accomplishment of a task – such as washing up, re-planting flowers or using a mobile phone to send an SMS. Other practices – such as those of debating or writing – are equally embodied and involve movements even though they might be seen as linguistic practices. Practices such as imagining while gazing out of the window, watching television sitting on the sofa or listening to the radio can likewise be understood as being in movement. This is possible because the notion of movement I am using here refers to the idea of movement as a way of moving forward. Following Massey (2005: 124) we cannot 'go back' either in our imaginations or in our footsteps. What we do and the materialities we encounter in the present have always moved on and are always in the process of moving on. Therefore when we research what people are doing while they are in the act of doing it, we are always focusing on how they are moving in and through the world, and how in doing so they are at the same time uniquely making something of that world and something of themselves.

In some circumstances the processes through which practices are learnt and the contexts in which they are experienced are much less social, sometimes solitary, or embedded in intimate forms of sociality that do not invite researcher presence. Domestic learning is one of these contexts. Many researchers might have in their own lifetimes participated as a form of apprentice to domestic practices, even if passively or without active attention to the practice. Yet the types of relationships, longitudinal timescales and levels of intrusion that the becoming of a domestic apprentice entails, makes it difficult to include this in an ethnographic project. Yet there are other routes to exploring such practices. One is the researcher's own domestic auto-ethnography. An early example of this emerges from the literature on everyday life studies in the work of Luce Giard. As part of her work with Michel de Certeau on the practices of everyday life, Giard (1998a, b) reflects on her biographical experiences of cooking and learning to cook. While as a younger person Giard had 'resisted' learning to cook as a process of attentive and gendered domestic apprenticeship, she later decided to teach herself using cookbooks. This process enabled her to understand the embodied learning that she had accrued in the past, as she writes: 'I had to admit that I too had been provided with a woman's knowledge and that it had crept into me, slipping past my mind's surveillance' (Giard 1998a: 153). Yet Giard, in line with the arguments made by de Certeau (1984), insists that resistance is central to the practice of cooking. Another way to develop auto-ethnography is through domestic diaries of one's own everyday practices. As an experiment in this I have reflected on my own domestic energy use practices, showing how the interweaving of different sets of practices and values forms part of a short everyday trajectory between waking up and starting work in the morning (Pink 2011d). The auto-ethnographer nevertheless has a limited sample. Giard also interviewed women about their experiences. And in my own work the everyday energy use narrative was used as a starting point for considering how to approach researching other people's everyday energy use.

To focus closely on practice as it is lived in homes, I have used a method that combines researcher video recording and participant reflection on a specific practice. This method might also include detailed verbal and audio-recorded interviews, yet it goes beyond the interview in that it engages the embodied practice itself in the process through which it is discussed. It also entails elements of learning in that the research participant is showing the researcher how the practice is performed. As such the researcher is learning about rather than *in doing* the practice. Yet such methods also involve the empathetic embodied engagements of researchers. When we attentively watch another person undertaking an activity that we are seeking to learn about the experience of, we use our own biographical embodied experiences to empathetically imagine what the experience of the other person is. This is not to say that we can imagine the same experience. Yet it does imply a process of non-verbal embodied learning. This method can be referred to as video (re)enactment – it involves the performance of everyday practices, yet it is important to acknowledge that they are enacted specifically as part of a research event, rather than being observed happening as they would as everyday life is routinely lived out. Yet I argue that the focus on (re)enactment as a method of accessing practicalities and memories about how practices are performed and a concern with how practices *are actually practiced* allows us to understand more closely the sensory and affective dimensions of practice, and following from this the roles they play in the constitution of place.

In Chapters 4 and 5, which focus on the detail of practice, I discuss everyday practices of kitchen cleaning and washing up and laundry, both of which were researched in part using the video (re)enactment method. Chapter 6 takes a different route to exploring practice. Here, rather than asking participants to (re)enact practices, I invited them to discuss and recount practices related to community gardening, while situated in material and sensory contexts that were the outcomes of such practices. As I describe in Chapter 7, I also participated in activist events and committee meetings, as well as following reported events through their representations. In these chapters the analytical focus itself shifts further from the detail of practice towards the flows and experiences that constitute place, and the ways in which new material and sensory configurations can facilitate shifts in practice. For the research that is discussed in Chapter 8, different methods were engaged. Here the focus of the analysis is on representations and web platform materials that are both the outcomes of digital activist practices and participants in the practices of users. In Chapter 2, I suggested that a focus on practice offers one route in to understanding processes of everyday life, resistance, activism and social change. The ways in which we research practice have an inevitable impact on the sorts of understandings that can be derived from our investigations. This is demonstrated as we move through Chapters 4–8 where the relationship of the researcher to the performance of practices, the environments in which they are performed and the representations that emerge from them, gradually shifts.

RESEARCHING REPRESENTATIONS IN MOVEMENT

In cultural studies there is a well-established tradition of the study of everyday life through the analysis of its representation in a range of media. Moran, for example, takes the approach that the everyday can be 'read' through the analysis of existing texts (2005: 25). Such an approach involves the analysis of everyday life *through* its representation, rather than in terms of its phenomenological reality. Thus focusing on representations as 'disparate sources', Moran suggests: 'This approach might help to denaturalize a quotidian time, that so often seems continuous and interminable' (2005: 26). He describes it with reference to a series of photographs of a bus route made by the photographer Tom Wood: 'What is really interesting about Wood's project is not the *punctum* of the individual images but the slow-burning, cumulative effect of the series as a whole' (Moran 2005: 26, original italics). This, according to Moran, allows 'the patient viewer to re-examine the overlooked surfaces of quotidian life' (2005: 26). Such treatments of representations as text to be read indeed invite viewers to imagine the rhythms, sensations and experiences of other people's everyday lives. There is undeniably a relationship between everyday life as lived and everyday life as represented. Moreover, representation is a part of everyday life, and integral to the mediation of everyday life encounters as digital media and communications technologies are increasingly part of our everyday social and technological worlds. Yet, as I have suggested above, in the context of a sensory turn in research practice, a semiotic approach to the reading of everyday life through representations also has its limits. In this book I also work with texts that are part of everyday life, yet I explore a different treatment of them within the research process. In agreement with theorists of practice whose work I discussed in Chapter 2, I argue that meanings are not held and cannot be sought through the analysis of texts as representation. Yet along with cultural studies scholars of everyday life I would argue for attending to representations. I propose under-standing meaning as produced through the relationality of texts and representations with other things, in practice and as part of place. In doing so I build on the work of Ingold, who offers some interesting insights regarding the potentiality of representations. Ingold questions the visual culture studies approach to drawings and paintings and sug-gests that we might approach them as being '*like* things in the world' rather than '*of* things in the world'. Following this we would 'have to find our ways through and among them, inhabiting them as we do the world itself' (Ingold 2010a: 16, original italics). Ingold's ideas offer a way of departing from the semiotic focus on analysing images and their content, while still recognising that visual images play a role in the world. My methodological interest is in how we might under-stand the role of representations in the processes through which mean-ings emerge in their intersections with practices. Therefore, in the following chapters, my focus on texts is twofold. First, I am concerned with their status as the outcomes of everyday life or activist practices – of photographing, video recording, drawing, writing, and more. Second, I am interested in their capacity as participants in the practices and places of everyday life and activism, for instance, in being involved in the constitution of place, and in the practices of memory and imagination.

On one level this accommodates an understanding of representations as emergent *from* rather than simply as standing for or inviting viewers to imagine practices, places and experiences. For example, in Chapter 7, I incorporate into the discussion an analysis of how local sustainabil-ity activists use and engage with representations and material objects ranging from analogue to digital photographs, posters, web pages, road traffic speed limit signs and plastic bags. Further, I discuss how photo-graphs and new materialities can become part of (digital and material) environments where they are engaged in the constitution of memories and urban identities. In the same chapter I also demonstrate how, through my own participation in an event with a video camera, I produced video, not as a representation of an event, but as a trail through that event, its socialities and activities. This approach is put into practice further in the analysis in Chapter 8, where I shift the focus away from the analysis of ethnographic encounters with domestic practitioners, gardeners and activists developed in the earlier chapters, and towards a discussion of encounters with digital media representa-tions on web platforms. This move away from the detail of everyday practice requires us to think in terms of everyday life in places that combine online and material encounters. Elsewhere (Pink 2012) I discuss how, to date, in Internet studies places have been interpreted first, by Christine Hine, in a Web 1.0 context as connected by what Manuel Castells (1996) has called the 'space of flows' (Hine 2000: 85) and more recently by Tom Boellstorff through a phenomenological approach to suggest that in the three-dimensional Web (based on his ethnography of second life) one is able to gain 'a sense of place' (2008: 91), on the basis of which he argues that there are 'online places' (2008: 92). However, in Chapter 2, I proposed a rather different definition of place, which informs the face-to-face everyday life research methods I have discussed in the earlier sections of this chapter. This notion of place departs from the idea that places have specific qualities that lend a sense of place to them, and are necessarily identified with material mappable localities, or online localities. As I have argued elsewhere in more detail (Pink 2012), this methodology is also suggestive for the way we might conceive the idea of online places. Thus online places can be seen as environments that we participate in as we *move through* the Web (rather than as places that we can *go to* online) and as multi-sensory. Simultaneously online ethnographers are thus involved in the process of making online places through their own media practices and as part of digital ecologies that span online and offline worlds, thus creating what I have elsewhere called 'ethnographic places' (Pink 2009a). They are also involved in encounters with both the experiential and representational. In Internet ethnography, this is perhaps most obvious in that we encounter digital media that have identifiable content (for example written or visual) and that we experience through our bodies and senses.

As a digital researcher one encounters the Internet and related tech-nologies and platforms in a way that, to borrow Massey's (2005: 141) phrase, can be understood as an engagement with a 'constellation of processes'. This includes a convergence or interweaving of online and offline processes, technological, biographical and representational and involving multiple media. Methodologically one of the interesting elements of the Internet is that it is multimedia and thus involves its user in a series of encounters with representations of different kinds. Yet, as I demonstrate in Chapter 8, rather than analysing these representations as texts that can be 'read', my concern is to interrogate their relationality and acknowledge that they invite sensory, embodied and affective encounters between viewer/researcher and the persons, ideas and things represented.

CONCLUSION

In this chapter I have proposed a methodology for researching everyday life and activism that accounts for practices, places and representations.

This necessitates a reflexive appreciation of the practices of the researcher and the places of which these become a part. It requires us to understand how we as researchers *move* through, experience and participate in research contexts and how as the producers and consumers of representations we are involved in both creating and exploring images and texts that simultaneously tell about and are part of the everyday and activism.

4

BEYOND DOING THE DISHES: PUTTING KITCHEN PRACTICES IN PLACE

Imagine a man in his early thirties, approaching his kitchen sink, leaning backwards slightly to accommodate the sloping wall of his attic flat, which inclined over the sink. It looked, as he put it, 'very tricky [because] … you have to stand like this and bend knees which means you don't want to stand here for too long'. A friend had considered moving in to share the flat with him but, he told me, 'She said she wouldn't do that because of the kitchen sink. The kitchen sink was the thing that stopped it in the end. It was the clincher but she wasn't sure anyway'. As I continued video recording, he washed up a glass, and placed it on the window ledge just to his right, which he had covered in pieces of grey slate creating a smooth cool surface. This was, he said: 'Because it catches the light and looks nicer, yes. I think it's also out of the way.'

As this description suggests, everyday practical activity in modern Western kitchens involves complex human perception of and purposeful engagements in an aesthetic, material, sensory, social and power-infused environment. In the social sciences, domestic activities are increasingly conceptualised through theories of practice and as multisensorial. In this chapter I expand on the theme of situating practices in relation to place as developed in Chapter 2, to explore how everyday life practices in the kitchen are implicated in the making of place. My focus is on how a man and a woman, both white and British, of similar ages and living in the UK, renew their kitchens through everyday housework practices. I attend to differences in the detail of how individual practitioners both engage in the multisensory practices of washing up and kitchen cleaning and to how they verbalise their experiences, feelings and beliefs around this practice. This understanding, I argue, is essential for interpreting how practices shift and change and has implications for comprehending the nature of practice as potentially innovative and transformative. It can therefore inform an understanding of the potential of creating interventions that support sustainability agendas.

INTRODUCTION

In a celebration of everyday domestic life, de Certeau's collaborator Luce Giard argued that 'such life activities demand as much intelligence, imagination and memory as those traditionally held as superior, such as music and weaving. In this sense, they rightly make up one of the strong aspects of ordinary culture' (Giard 1998a: 151). The study of domestic life had a strong appeal for everyday life scholars in their agenda to reveal the significance of hidden routines and pleasures. While less frequently linked to this earlier work, interest in everyday housework, home decoration and cooking practices has endured in the arts and social sciences.

Sociological engagements with practice theory are becoming increasingly influential in the study of domestic consumption (see Halkier et al. 2011). In this chapter, following the argument developed in Chapter 2, I develop an interdisciplinary approach to comment on the implications of situating this practice focus on domestic life in relation to theoretical and ethnographic elaborations of place and sensory knowing and perception. In doing so I engage the theoretical and methodological approach to the senses discussed in Chapter 1 and to understanding practice *in practice* and in relation to place as outlined in Chapters 2 and 3, thus demonstrating how this approach invites us to reconfigure our understandings of domestic environments, the processes through which they are constituted and the potentialities of practice. These shifts have already had some impact on existing scholarship across anthropology and sociology whereby the home and domestic practices are re-conceptualised as multisensory (Pink 2004), domestic food preparation is analysed via theories of 'skilled practice, the senses and memory' (Sutton 2006: 87) and domestic design, consumption and its materiality might be understood through combining theories of practice and material agency (Shove et al. 2007). In this chapter, I build on these literatures to understand the kitchen by situating the material, sensory and affective experiences, qualities and agencies of practice in relation to a theory of place. This, I suggest, enables an understanding of how everyday practices, localities and things converge in the making of kitchens and selves.

To consider practice *in practice* I reflect on two examples from a video ethnography of washing up and kitchen cleaning undertaken in collaboration with Unilever Research in 1999. In this research, practitioners both discussed the material, sensory and affective dimensions of their kitchens, and performed and reflected on their practice *in practice* (see Pink 2004), thus providing an example of the video (re) enactment method outlined in Chapter 3. I suggest that both routine (e.g. dishwashing) and occasional (e.g. home improvement, adding/ removing appliances) transformation of kitchens can be understood as occurring within a complex kitchen ecology constituted by persons and things in movement, and their material and memorial traces and imaginings. Thus the material objects and practices that might be considered as fundamental to kitchens cannot exist in isolation from what Ingold calls the 'meshwork' of place (2008). Implicit in this suggestion is the caution against conflating practice with simply 'doing' and place with material 'locality'. On the one hand, this approach shows how conventions are followed so that the participants can be said to be engaging in an identifiable practice called 'washing up'. Yet simultaneously it reveals the detail of how innovation is produced through the performance of practice, as well as the ways in which this is contingent on the wider environment. In some ways this resonates with Giard's earlier work on the French kitchen, where she described cooking as 'a domain where tradition and innovation matter equally' (1998a: 151). As I have argued elsewhere (Pink 2004), while domestic practices can be engaged to sustain conventional moralities, values and ways of being, they are also frequently sites for developing innovations that depart from what domestic practitioners understand as traditional ways of doing, being and experiencing. In this chapter I show through these examples how at the intersection between practices of everyday life, their performances by different practitioners and other components of unique configurations may emerge normativity, innovation, change and thought-out activism, and that these are not necessarily separate from each other.

PERSPECTIVES ON DOMESTIC PRACTICE

In Chapter 2, I outlined how theories of practice and place are both contested and applied in diverse ways across the social sciences. In terms of their application to domestic contexts, likewise their use has not been entirely consistent. Nevertheless some key strands emerging from sociology and anthropology offer a starting point for understanding how everyday life in the home can be understood through a focus on practice. The earlier bodies of work in this area tended to focus on gendered housework roles (e.g. Oakley 1974 [1985], Beer 1983, and see Pink 2004 for a review of this), cooking as an everyday practice (de Certeau 1984, Giard 1998a) and the study of material culture in relation to the constitution of self identity (Miller 1988, 2001, Clarke 2001). Moreover, domestic practices are inescapably bound up with the self-identities, biographies and imaginations of those who perform them (see also Miller 1998, 2001, Pink 2004, Sutton 2006). Thus showing how our understanding domestic practices as collective or as 'entities' (Schatzki 2001, Warde 2005, Shove et al. 2007) and as modified when performed, is also necessarily tied up with the way that the specificity of the performance of practices is interwoven with processes of self. One way to frame this was developed in the work of Giard and de Certeau. Here, Giard, with a firm commitment to the idea of domestic practice as a site for resistance, has argued that 'Between the symmetrical errors of archaistic nostalgia and frenetic overmodernisation, room remains for microinventions, for the practice of *reasoned differences,* to resist with a sweet obstinance the contagion of conformism, to reinforce the network of exchanges and relations, to learn how to make one's own choice among the tools and commodities produced by the industrial era' (Giard 1998b: 213, original italics). As I argued in Chapter 2, treating the practice of everyday life as one that is *essentially* concerned with resistance would be an exaggeration. Yet, as Warde (2005) has shown, the possibility and potential for change, or thinking more in Marchand's (2010) terms, innovation, is inseparable from everyday practice. Therefore there may be elements of practices that are collectively performed and a practice might be defined as an 'entity'. As the examples in this chapter show, we can identify both as being cases of the practice of dish washing. Yet when actually performed the structure of a practice as it is defined when abstracted may be diverted by innovative twists. Thus, to achieve, for example, social or design interventions that enable people to develop sustainable practice in their homes, an understanding of the nature of practice as experienced, performed, shifting and innovative would be needed.

Existing research about everyday domestic practices and places offers some key inroads. Anthropological studies of the home have been influenced by the material culture approach developed by Danny Miller. In a seminal article in this area, focusing on the kitchen and published in 1988, Miller outlined a theory of alienation and appropriation. His research with 40 people living on a council estate, examined 'how essentially identical facilities provided by the council have been differentially employed in the long term' (Miller 1988: 356). Miller's research was about how different households had decorated their kitchens in ways that enabled them to feel more or less alienated from their homes. Their actions can also be interpreted as creating a quality of home by appropriating specific areas of the home designated as the kitchen. In Chapter 2 I noted how, by drawing on practice theory, Shove et al.'s work (2007) has moved the debate in a different direction to demonstrate that practice, material agency and imagination are inextricable in the processes through which kitchens are constituted. By combining practice theory with understandings of material agency, Shove et al. propose how domestic practices and materialities change. With specific reference to the kitchen, they suggest that 'things are acquired, discarded and redesigned with reference to culturally and temporally specific expectations of doing *and* of having – not of having alone' (2007: 37,original italics). Yet these insights also imply further questions, which concern the experiential, sensory, affective and embodied aspects of kitchen materialities and practices (including practices of memory and imagination) *and* how these are part of wider kitchen ecologies. Such concerns are not beyond the scope of theories of practice, as Warde sums up: 'Practice theories comprehend non-instrumentalist notions of conduct, both observing the role of routine on the one hand, and emotion, embodiment and desire on the other' (2005: 136). Indeed Shove et al. recognise the significance of 'competence, skill and effective accomplishment' (2007: 38). However, as Sutton has pointed out, 'there has been relatively little research on consumption as not simply a creative, but a *skilled* process, involving judgement and the reasoned use of the senses' (2006: 88). In this sense, such approaches from phenomenological and sensory anthropology and sociological approaches to practice, should be able to usefully inform each other. As I argue elsewhere, social scientists can benefit from understanding the home as 'a site of sensory consumption' (Pink 2007d: 164) and from an appreciation of the sensory (as well as material) agencies of home (Pink 2004). As Sutton's work also demonstrates in relation to food preparation, domestic tasks involve skilled practices and tacit, sensory embodied ways of knowing that are as much located in domestic social and power relations as being related to material agencies. Following Ingold's point that 'skilled practice involves … a mobilization of the mind/body within an environment of "objects" which "afford" different possibilities for human use' (Sutton 2006: 91), Sutton analyses cooking practices as they are demonstrated by research participants *in practice*. He argues for attentiveness to 'both the "technical" skills and sensory aspects of cooking, and its more explicitly social dimensions' (2006: 110). Likewise, through the concept of the 'sensory home' (Pink 2004), I have understood domestic contexts as configured in relation to intersections between material and human agencies, along with discourses on moralities, individual identities and the sensory/social/material production of 'home' through everyday housework and home decoration practices. Sutton's (2006) and my own (2004) observations thus suggest that to understand practices related to the kitchen requires a theory that extends the focus on materiality and practice, to understand how this wider complex or constellation of things, discourses, sensations, skills, ways of knowing and practices cohere and are indeed in part, at least, mutually constituting. This leads me to the question of how then might one abstract the idea of a kitchen and what happens in it theoretically? In what follows I explore this through a concept of place.

WHAT IS A KITCHEN? THE ENTANGLEMENT OF (DOMESTIC) PLACE

I now return to the question of the distinction between the notions of the kitchen on the one hand as a locality and on the other hand as a place. This allows me to reflect on the implications of the above discussion for defining kitchens as places and subsequently for defining kitchen practices.

As I noted above, the materiality of the kitchen has been emphasised in existing literature (e.g. Miller 1988, Shove et al. 2007). Here I build on this to understand the kitchen through a further set of qualities. From a theoretical perspective, a kitchen is not a material or mapped locality. Rather it is a place in Massey's sense of being a form of 'event' (2005: 130). Moreover, if we follow Ingold (2008) to see place as an entanglement, a kitchen might represent the intensity of things, practices and more that come together in particular ways – whose 'lines' (Ingold 2007) become interwoven or enmeshed. This formulation is not simply a theoretical speculation. While in the examples discussed below modern Western architectural definitions of a kitchen largely coincide with those of the research participants, as in the example with which I began this chapter, material structures and practical activities are not always perfectly matched. This point is illustrated well in Martens' work on kitchen practices. Martens quotes a participant who describes how, when his family moved into their home, the kitchen was 'not useable at all'. Particularly significant is that Martens quotes him relating that 'it was very old units, everything was dirty, the floor was horrible. Everything was horrible in the kitchen. There was no way we could cook in this kitchen. *It was like having no kitchen*' (Martens 2007: 42, my italics). When this happens kitchens may be refurbished. However, in other circumstances, as Sally Booth's (1999) example of Sicilian women who had been re-housed after an earthquake shows, when practitioners find architecturally defined kitchens inappropriate to their existing practices, they might not use them as kitchens. In the case of Booth's research, the women relocated their kitchens to areas intended for use as garages. This enabled them to maintain the socialities and other conditions that for them constituted the *quality* of a kitchen. To theorise these contexts requires an understanding not only of the kitchen as place but of the human and material agencies that are both part of or involved in the constitution of the constellations of things that are kitchens. There are indeed certain practices and material consumer objects that are expected in a modern Western kitchen. However (as already illustrated above through Martens' [2007] work) for a kitchen to be a kitchen, and for a person to call it 'my kitchen' in a way that draws together self and locality, many other things are also involved, including skills, knowing, moralities, desires, socialities and the right embodied sensations in relation to it.

Therefore, while in part kitchens are constituted through an intersection between human practices, materialities and their respective agencies, they are also more than this. If we think of kitchens as being sensed through the bringing together of (unbounded) constellations or intensities of things in movement, we can consider how within this, practices, materialities and self-identities are essential and dynamic elements. Indeed they are produced and constantly change in this continuous process of movement. This does not of course mean that kitchens are *experienced* as fast-moving, changing events. Indeed it is through routinised practices that people maintain and can thus gain a *sense of* the stability of kitchens. Rather, a theory of place offers us a framework to understand the environments that practices are both part of and involved in the constantly shifting constitution of. It enables us to define a kitchen as place-event rather than as a material, architecturally inscribed locality. Within this process, human practitioners define kitchens subjectively and in culturally specific ways, as having a series of qualities.

RESEARCHING KITCHEN PRACTICE *IN PRACTICE*

I have argued that domestic practices are multisensory (Pink 2004), (domestic) consumption is a sensory and '*skilled* process' (Sutton 2006: 88, original italics) and practices are inextricable from place. To support this idea requires a research methodology based in a reflexive investigation of practices *in practice* and *as part of place*, thus making an analysis of practice in place a route to understanding domestic transformations as changing constellations of intensities to which human and material agencies are integral. As I argued in Chapter 3, if theory is to be matched with empirical investigation, the research methodology and theory must be mutually congruent. By understanding practice in relation to a theory of place, we can recognise not only materiality and the intersections between human and material agencies, but also the idea that practices are only ever lived out, modified or become obsolete as part of a wider constellation or ecology of things, conceptualised through Ingold's notion of place as a 'meshwork' (2008). While wider methodological issues were outlined in Chapter 3, here I focus on how these approaches can be mobilised in the pursuit of understanding everyday kitchen practices.

Commenting on Schatzki's (1996: 89) notion of practice as an entity involving 'sayings and doings', Warde points out this suggests 'that analysis must be concerned with both practical activity and its representation' (2005: 134). Indeed, researching kitchen practices *in practice* and *in place* involves a series of methodological challenges, which require going beyond conventional interviewing. In their work on kitchen practices, Martens and Scott note it is difficult for practitioners to represent practices through interviews and surveys, resolving this in their research through the installation of CCTV cameras in participants' kitchens, alongside interviewing methods (Martens and Scott 2004: 21). The examples I discuss below were researched as part of a project 'Cleaning Homes and Lifestyles', developed with Unilever Research in 1999, and focus on washing up and kitchen cleaning. The wider project involved in-depth interviews, domestic video tours and video-recorded cleaning practice demonstrations with 40 participants in Spain and England (see Pink 2004, 2006). The objective was not to attempt to record everyday kitchen practices as they are lived, but to collaboratively explore and reflect on the materiality of the kitchen and 'normal' routine everyday practices with participants. Thus focusing on the objects and traces that compose the kitchen and the usual performance of practices and questions including why they are done this way, what associations they might have with other persons, materialities, memories, aspirations and imagined futures, moralities and identities. By reflecting on practices and things while the participants were actually in embodied engagements in and with them, we were concurrently involved in a method of producing understandings.

I sought to understand these practices on the terms of their practitioners, and through not only verbal accounts but through embodied engagements. As Sutton's (2006) use of video in researching food preparation practices in the United States also shows, audiovisual recording can reveal both verbal and tacit embodied knowing in practice and representations of practice. Being aware that I was recording their practices enabled participants to show me (and 'the video') 'how' they did things, the material results of their practices and to reflect on the sensory (e.g. heat, smell, texture, visual, comfort or discomfort) and affective dimensions of the process (e.g. memories, desires, satisfaction, frustration, therapeutic qualities). On the one hand, the method might be interpreted as making verbalisations and embodied actions cohere in the research encounter. For instance, consider the difference between washing a glass and talking about how one does this. In modern Western culture making this differentiation is part of a conventional *practice of showing* others how things are done. But if we conflate both verbalising and enacting practices into the category of 'knowing', both activities can be understood as 'ways of knowing' – specifically ways of *knowing in practice*. The verbalisation around the activity cannot be extracted from the activity and in this instance is itself a practice. Thus what Warde calls 'practical activity and its representation' (2005: 134) become one and the same performance. This, I suggest, might be seen as an ethnographic route to understanding what Wenger calls 'knowing in practice' (1998). Finally we should acknowledge that (as developed in Pink 2009a) the place-event of the research encounter is also one that the researcher her or himself is part of, and is as such implicated in its constitution. In the case of the research encounters discussed below, the participants had each selected their task between kitchen and bathroom cleaning and as they performed the task they explained their actions to me while I sometimes probed further to invite them to reflect on biographical, memorial and experiential issues.

Next I focus on two British participants who performed and reflected on their washing up and kitchen cleaning practices with me. They were both working full time, in their early twenties and childless. Nicola lived alone, having previously shared houses when she was a student. Paul lived in a shared house. I focus on how they discuss and perform material objects, traces and washing up in practice.

THE PRACTICES AND PLACES OF WASHING UP: TWO INDIVIDUALS

NICOLA AND THE 'PROPER' KITCHEN

'This is the kitchen', announced Nicola as we passed through a small arch from the living room into a long narrow area furnished with cupboards and a work surface along one side, a sink below a window at one end and a fridge at the other. As we toured the room it became increasingly evident how this kitchen was a locality where materialities, technologies, sensory experiences, social relationships, moralities and everyday practices were 'entangled' to make a place.

One of Nicola's first points concerned the aesthetics of the kitchen and how its mainly matching appliances (which she had some control over, as it was a rented property) were implicated in this. She had been given a microwave but 'it was too ugly … [it] ruined my house'. Nicola combined words and body to show how its inappropriately 'industrial' size had occupied her kitchen surface, using her hands to map out the area. As she would use it only 'every now and again' she reflected that the trade-off of having such a 'monstrosity' in her house for the sake of having 'all mod cons' was too great. Kitchen designs and the localities that people call kitchens are not only determined through aesthetic practices and the intentional movement/removal of objects, but also through human movement, socialities and embodied actions. As the tour proceeded Nicola noted that her cooker was 'dirty' because a friend had fried a sandwich on it for her (something she would never do herself) the previous day, leaving a pan of oil and splashes on the surface. Nicola would have cleaned this the evening of the interview, but for now the material traces of this agency, sociality and the path her friend had taken through her kitchen remained. However, to this she attached a moral and aesthetic discourse. By way of contrast she reached down to a cupboard. Taking out a glass she assured me that *this* was guaranteed to be totally clean and promised to later show me how she washed up her glasses herself to ensure that they reached a certain standard of cleanliness. It is this 'constellation' (Massey 2005) of things in process that makes the kitchen a place. However, as I show below, cleanliness was not necessarily assessed though the visible evidence of the clean glass, but rather in the embodied knowing of the skilled practice of cleaning it.

A pile of washing up awaited us and Nicola demonstrated the normal procedure that she would follow. She rinsed out the washing up bowl, squirted in washing up liquid and filled it with water, and reflected on how she always uses too much detergent, resulting in a very bubbly composition. Nicola's practices are not simply idiosyncratic, but as 'entities' have some coherence with others when performed. Like other English research participants, she usually washed her glasses first. She explained this in terms of the feel of the washing up process, 'because otherwise everything gets greasy'. Nicola proceeded to wash a set of tall, thin water glasses. She reflected on her method, however, as personalised. While wiping the outside and inside of the glasses, she noted how you need small hands to be able to clean them in this way. As she rinsed off the soap, holding the glass at the end, she pointed out that this part of the process required very hot water, and I noticed how the movements of her hands were designed to avoid too much contact between the water and her skin itself as she commented that 'I burn myself sometimes when I do this'. In the past Nicola had worn rubber gloves, which enabled her to use even hotter water. She had 'got out of the habit' because the gloves kept getting holes in them and she had not replaced them. Here it becomes clear how technologies, the senses, skill and knowing in practice and human and material agencies begin to intersect in the process of kitchen renewal. As Nicola restores her glasses to a clean state, an intensity of contact between a series of elements of a kitchen ecology is brought about – including energy, heat, water, bubbles, glass, hands, knowing, skill and moral discourses. The glasses were left to drain in a rack on the draining board next to the sink. Statements about self-identity were never far from the way participants in this research talked about their washing up practices. Nicola identified her own washing up practices as different to those of 'other people' who, she demonstrated by performing this with a glass, might simply wipe over the outside and leave it to dry without rinsing the soap suds off, on a bare draining board. However, this should be interpreted beyond the idea that self-identities are constituted through the performance of practices in the kitchen. Rather, it calls for an examination of the relationship between practices, of which identity is a part, of how people understand and experience kitchens as particular types of localities, and of how they attach moral standards to these. Nicola's glasses bear the traces of her agency, and thus become a materialisation of the morality and standards through which she defines and creates a 'proper' kitchen. However, this agency cannot be disassociated from the embodied, sensory, skilled 'knowing in practice' through which the glasses are cleaned or from the practices of memory and imagination that are part of this.

Nicola's example raises some key themes. First, we can see how the kitchen, although it corresponds with an architecturally defined, walled location, is determined as a 'proper' kitchen through a set of multisensory practices involving skilled ways of knowing that are engaged *in practice*. These practices also have moral dimensions and are concerned with the constitution of self-identity as well as with the renewal of a kitchen. The constant process of the destruction and renewal of the aesthetic and sensory state of standards in the kitchen involves the movement of things (e.g. the outgoing microwave and incoming actual and imagined artefacts, cleaning technologies such as gloves and bleach, water and energy), persons (e.g. Nicola and her friend) and discourses. As these things in process intersect with changing degrees of intensity, the kitchen as a place is constituted and re-constituted.

PAUL AND THE SHARED KITCHEN

As we walked into the kitchen of the rented terrace house Paul shared with other young professionals, he commented that it was 'remarkably cleaner than it usually is' – usually piled up with dirty pots and empty wine bottles. As his home was rented and shared, Paul's degree of knowledge about, investment in and engagement with the domestic interior and the maintenance of the kitchen was less than he anticipated it would be if he was an owner-occupier. In contrast to Nicola, Paul had less control over kitchen materialities and processes, and his own kitchen practices intersected with those of the other housemates. As we toured the kitchen with the camera, he identified changes in order and cleanliness made by others over the last couple of days – such as moving bottles in preparation for recycling. Looking at the cooker, which he told me was usually dirtier, he identified tin foil and a used tray left on top of the grill, explaining how a shared practice in the house of putting this and subsequent layers of foil on it would mean that it did not have to be washed up. He also showed me a cupboard where they had stored the items left by the previous occupants of the house, identified that people individually stored their food in their own cupboards and showed me his own shelf on the fridge. Particularly interesting was a stained area of the wall. This had happened through a shared practice of throwing teabags at the target of the bin, which either missed and hit the wall or splashed onto it on their way. Paul and other housemates had tried to clean this but could not remove the stains. This left material and memory traces of a series of practices as well as a way of understanding the kitchen through these practices. The kitchen was not thus identified as 'his' and he told me that if it was it would need to be 'gutted' and re-done. Paul nevertheless applied the skills and techniques (and embedded moralities) that he had learnt while living with his parents to washing up and surface cleaning, along with innovations specific to that particular social and material environment.

He began washing up by testing the temperature of the water from the tap, holding his hand underneath its flow, while boiling the kettle to produce more hot water. He explained that the water heater only heated a certain amount of water each day and in the shared house he lived in this was used up, leaving the remaining water 'cool' rather than icy cold. Once the kettle had boiled, he continued talking about how he felt about cleaning as he poured the hotter water into the bowl and tested the new temperature by dipping his fingers in the water and then adding more cold water, more boldly swishing around the warm bubbly mixture, explaining that he does not use gloves. Identifying glasses, cups and cutlery as being less dirty, he placed these first in the washing up water, pointing out that usually dirtier pots would be done later. Paul explained to me that he did not listen to music while washing up, as the TV in the living room would be on in the background normally, and it would not be worth bringing a stereo down just for that purpose. He washed up as we continued talking, wiping the items with a cloth, and in one case returning a spoon for further wiping after visually assessing it, before placing them on the draining board. After washing up he wiped over the surfaces. Pulling the dishcloth over to the edge he explained how his hand held below would fill with crumbs and bits, which he dropped into the bin. When I asked him how he knew it was clean he said it was because 'it looks clean', commenting that he had not really thought about how other elements figured in its cleanliness. Yet, as was evident in his actions, cleaning the kitchen had been a multisensory process, perhaps most explicitly involving tactile ways of knowing (about heat, smoothness of surfaces and the movement of a cloth over them, the consistency of bubbly water and more) as well as visual evaluation.

Like Nicola's example, Paul's demonstrates that the kitchen of his shared house is not simply a pre-existing locality that is created through the renewal of kitchen equilibrium though everyday practice. Rather, it is constituted as a place through an intensity of relationships between a set of people, material objects, and furnishings and actual practices, all of which are in movement and/or process. The qualities of the kitchen as place in this case are also created through domestic socialities and shared practices and innovations that emerged. Thus Paul's agency is negotiated in relation to that of others and *their* practices, moralities and standards. The materiality of the kitchen can at times be seen as a manifestation of this, as for instance in the case of the teabag-stained wall. The stains become both the traces of a practice and a constituent of place, and a material manifestation of moralities.

THE DETAIL OF PRACTICE

There are certain ways in which kitchen practices were consistent across most participants in my research (such as washing the glasses first or wiping over surfaces last) (see Pink 2004). While these are significant findings, my interest here is not in these practices as artefacts or units that can be analysed, that is, in treating them as entities that exist as a meta-narrative to the phenomenology of practice. Rather, I am concerned with treating the performance of practices as lived manifestations of and modifiers of skilled ways of knowing. A meta-view of practice that attends to the similarities in the practices people report verbally at any one point in historical time, can offer important insights into, for instance, the ways practices change in socio-technical-historical process. However, approaching the question of everyday practice through a focus on the specificity of practices as practised (or *in practice*) within particular constellations of place, offers a route to charting and understanding the complexities and variations in everyday life.

For example, both Nicola and Paul washed their glasses first. Yet the ways in which they did this and the discourses and biographical processes they invested in this were rather different. In Paul's kitchen cleaning practices, he sought to adhere to the moral standards he associated with his clean family home. For Nicola, in contrast, her methods of cleaning glasses were directly associated with not leaving the soapsuds on as others do, and her cleaning was situated as a departure from her family home. Moreover the embodied skills used for washing the glasses that had been developed and employed by both participants were different. Above I have described Nicola's use of very hot water and the techniques she used to avoid burning her skin. Each participant had different access to hot water and subsequently also used it differently in the ways they washed up. Nicola's hot water was not shared and she had no concern about there not being enough. In contrast Paul had to boil the kettle to supplement the hot water that was available in his shared home. To categorise the practice of washing up the glasses first, therefore, as a relevant finding would therefore only be informative on a very superficial level. It tells us very little about the innovations in washing the glasses that people make, or about the forms of convention they break or sustain in the performance of these practices. As the examples of Nicola and Paul also reveal, without attending to the details of and individual differentiations between the social, technological and temporal components of everyday life in the home, we would not learn about how heating water and other domestic energy uses are implicated in these processes, which, for research that is concerned with sustainability is a vital question.

In contrast, a focus on the detail of practice and the ways it is interwoven with biography, memory and morality can show us how and where the multiple potentials of practice for innovation, or for the maintenance of conventions might emerge, and illuminate the other constituents of place with which it becomes entangled.

PRACTICE AND SENSORY KNOWING IN PLACE

Both Nicola's and Paul's (shared) kitchens can be understood as being constituted through what Ingold (2008) refers to as the 'entanglement' of things that move, at different rates, creating intensities through their mutual presences and co-engagements. Indeed it is not only the *presence* of persons, things, sensations and more, but the *traces* created or left by them (whether these are affective memories, teabag stains, tins of beans or self-disciplining standards) that continue to constitute the kitchen–place–event. When both Nicola and Paul showed me their kitchens they were concerned with both the material, aesthetic and sensory presence of objects and with their traces. They told me and showed me, using their words, and whole bodies in movement, how these realities and traces were related to memories, moralities, standards and how they were *in practice* achieved or otherwise emerged. As such, the kitchen as a lived locality was defined by them through its materiality, its sensoriality and through their personal abilities and agency to maintain it according to their desires.

Modern Western practitioners are most likely to think of washing up and surface cleaning as things they do *in* and *to* the kitchen, or at least *to* objects *in* the kitchen in order to restore the kitchen to an appropriate standard of cleanliness. However, it is interesting to turn this idea on its head to think of what they do in the kitchen again as part of the process of making the kitchen-place. Therefore to understand practice as part of a kitchen-place, a focus on skilled (and moral) practice enables us to see how identity and practice are fused in the process whereby places come into being and are defined as particular 'types' of place. Thus certain practices, combined with the movements and traces of objects and things, might create a 'proper' or a 'tatty' kitchen in the terms of the research participant. Nicola told me that washing up in a different way would not be right 'for my glasses' and 'in my kitchen'. It is her sensory knowing in practice that informs her that the glasses are properly washed up. And this leads her to define the kitchen as properly 'her' kitchen through the idea of the cleanliness of the glasses. Here identities and moralities become bound up with knowing in practice, and localities become defined in practitioners' terms as certain types of room. In this sense, the kitchen-place as it is lived and experienced is always specific. But it is not fixed, therefore it is always changing, always open and is, in any one moment, determined through the entanglement of things, traces, sensations, moralities, skilled practices and more.

Existing social science uses of practice theories to understand human– material relations in the kitchen have emphasised the intersection between human and material agencies (Shove et al. 2007) and the centrality of skill and sensory knowing in practice (Sutton 2006). In this chapter I have suggested that, following work in human geography, practice is usefully understood in relation to a theory of place (e.g. Cresswell 2003) and that the notion of place as entanglement (Ingold 2008) offers a useful understanding of this. To reiterate my point, a theory of place allows us to understand kitchen practices as part of a kitchen ecology constituted through movements of persons and things (which include practices), rather than as something that is done in a priori determined localities. The further implications of this approach open up ways of thinking about kitchen practices in terms of wider issues. Two examples of this are questions about the relationship between the intimate context of the home and global flows, and questions relating to domestic energy consumption and sustainability.

GLOBAL FLOWS AND ACTIVISM IN THE KITCHEN

I have suggested that the kitchen should be seen as an 'open' or unbounded place. Massey's (2005) formulation of the relationship between place and space, however, offers a further insight as it suggests that we think of kitchens as places that are implicated in the politics of space. This approach invites us to consider how (global) flows are involved in processes through which skilled practices (and the discourses, moralities and more embedded in them) are implicated in the detail of domestic human–material–sensorial intersections. It moreover invites considerations of how kitchen (consumption) practices are implicated in global flows and processes – both in unanticipated ways and as forms of activist agency intended to have impacts beyond the immediate kitchen. The activism of the Slow movement (discussed further in Chapters 7 and 8) provides an interesting example here. Slow Food is an eco-gastronomic movement, with, among other things, a focus on environmental sustainability and local produce. As I have shown above, the performance of kitchen practices is contingent on a series of other constituents of place, including moralities, identities, hot water supplies, materialities, sensory experiences and skills. Kitchen practices are also interwoven with explicit discourses about (for example) the 'proper', 'ethical' and 'hygienic' ways to do things. Even if they are consciously aware of such discourses, people do not always inform the way they perform their practices with their principles. Yet in some cases, flows of knowledge, principles and activism are interwoven in how tasks are performed in kitchens. These subsequently have implications not only for the ways that practices shift and change, but also for the impacts of these shifts in practice. As Sue, who was a member of the Slow Food movement, described:

> I'm in heaven at the moment because it's asparagus season, in three of four weeks time that will be it. I will eat no more asparagus for a year and when the next season comes along it will be that moment of, it's asparagus again. And it's getting people back to that sort of thinking about food, rather than I fancy some asparagus and I don't mind if its been flown all the way from Peru. I actually do now mind because it can't be as good as when I can buy it cut that morning from my local village, so we don't have anything that's particularly distinctive but what we do is we do have very good quality.

Sue's practices were informed by the discourses of an Italian-based social movement, and at the same time are central to her own identity statements. They are also, however, interesting in that by ascribing to the principles of Slow Food they ensure that the flows to her kitchen follow certain routes – those of local produce emerging from local producers, which in turn influences what is cooked there. In Chapters 6 and 7, I develop further this discussion of how the activism of the Slow movement is implicated in the practices and places of everyday life through an analysis of the neighbourhood and the town. As this example shows, however, it also informs the way everyday life is lived in the kitchen.

THE SPECIFICITY OF PRACTICE AND ITS IMPLICATIONS FOR SUSTAINABILITY

The examples discussed above have a further significance in that they point to the detail of practice and the other constituents of place that define its performance as being essential to our understanding of how people both source the products they consume and the ways they use energy in their homes. As I have argued, it is not enough just to know that people usually wash their glasses first or that they attach a particular moral and practical value to doing so. Rather, the sensory embodied skills that individuals develop for this purpose, the identities they construct around this and the precise ways in which they engage these in relation to different domestic technologies and their affordances for heating water, might produce rather different levels of energy consumption between different households. Because these practices have some similarities in their definition but are not enacted in ways that are consistently normative, the realities of domestic energy consumption and routes to sustainability are both inevitably 'messy'. Yet if successful social and technological interventions are to be made to lead to a more sustainable society, we need ways to research, represent and deal with this diversity that will be appropriate to the social, affective, material and sensory emplacement of domestic practitioners. In the next chapter, I take the question of domestic energy consumption and flows further through a discussion of domestic laundry in movement.

CONCLUSION

In this chapter, I have argued for a fine-grained focus on the detail of domestic practice as it is situated in relation to place. Through the examples of individual practice, I have shown how domestic practices are redefined in their performance. They are essentially neither normative nor resistant but might combine elements of each and are likely to manifest different degrees of innovation. The impacts the performance of washing up and kitchen cleaning practices might have on the ways products are purchased and used and on sustainability agendas that seek to decrease domestic energy consumption are uneven. This, I argue, is a fundamental reason why it is important to recognise not simply that individual practitioners do things differently, but that the detail of why they do so is embedded within the complexity of the environmental conditions in which they perform practices. Once we situate the detail of everyday practice as such, in relation to place, we can access an analytical route that enables an understanding of the wider ecologies from which individual difference emerges.

5

MAKING THE SENSORY HOME: LAUNDRY ROUTES AND ENERGY FLOWS

I began my encounter with Jean in her beamed cottage living room. We had a quick chat before beginning our audio-recorded interview. In this case the interview should not be interpreted simply as a verbal exchange. Rather, settling down to the interview, drinking the coffee Jean had made me, sitting on her chair, I began to soak up the whole environment of her cosy living room, with its textures and ornaments. I sought to identify the smell and hairs of the dog that Jean told me were ever-present, wittily warning me that 'someone [like me, the ethnographer] comes in with a black skirt on and they go out with a dog coloured skirt'. To combat the smell of the dog, Jean used a standard product that improved the smell of the carpet when vacuuming. Yet the very presence of the dog deterred her from changing the now ageing carpets, since a new one would also be spoilt by him. However, the textures and environment of the room were controlled through laundry practices, for example, with the curtains washed about once a year. We discussed Jean's own preference for comfortable clothes and T-shirts, partly influenced by her dislike of ironing, and desire to limit the need for it. As we later toured the room with the video camera, Jean explained how to keep warm in the winter they would partition off the half of the room that they have the fireplace in, and told me about their plans to have more wooden textures. In the winter, laundry would also periodically create a whole new atmosphere in the living room when it was too cold and wet to peg out in the garden and it needed to be dried in front of the fire. At this point in our tour, laundry was already playing a role in my understanding of the sensory home in that we constantly encountered laundry items that were in progress. By this I mean items that were in the living room or its cupboards that had just been or that would become laundry as part of a cycle of washing. This included cushions, curtains, rugs and outdoor clothing. While we do not usually think of these things as laundry, they are in fact sensory – tactile, visual, olfactory – elements of home that are renewed and in research participants' terms 'refreshed' as part of a process through which the multisensory home is (re)constituted. Thinking about the sensory home through the prism of laundry offers an interesting route to consider how not only the feel, smell and visual presentation of home is achieved, but how domestic energy – such as gas and electricity – is consumed in the processes of washing, drying and ironing, and how these processes themselves make the sounds, smells, textures and visuality of the home.

INTRODUCTION

Building on the analysis developed in Chapter 4, this chapter advances the notion of the sensory home (Pink 2004) through an analysis of the practices, flows and movement, materialities and sensoriality of domestic laundry processes, as they traverse the home. It demonstrates how a domestic aesthetic can be conceptualised as part of a constantly shifting place-event constituted through constellations of these everyday things and mundane practices. Laundry is already established in sociological work as a route through which to study domestic processes. For instance, in France, the sociologist Jean-Claude Kaufmann examined gendered relationships in the home, seeing laundry as 'the tool – something that enables us to expose the underlying fabric of conjugal life' (Kaufmann 1998: 11) and laundry has been identified as a route to studying domestic energy consumption in both Britain and Denmark (e.g. Shove 2003, Gram-Hanssen 2008).

In the latter part of this chapter I draw on materials produced with five interview and video tour participants from an applied visual ethnography project I undertook in 2000, concerned with domestic laundry processes and practices. In contrast to the young professionals who featured in Chapter 4, all are middle-aged women. Alice was a full-time housewife, and Jane, Angela, Jean and Helen worked part-time, shaping their jobs flexibly around family life. Some of these materials are the same as those analysed by Shove (2003), but from a rather different perspective. Shove frames her analysis as exploring 'some of the processes involved in overturning and sustaining routine and habit' (2003: 140). In contrast I write from the perspective of the implicated researcher whose embodied situatedness remains in my (re)visiting of the research context through these materials (see Chapter 3). I explore how a phenomenological approach that situates practice in relation to place and follows the movement of people and things can tell a complementary story.

ENERGY ISSUES AND SCHOLARSHIP AROUND THE HOME

There exists a growing body of energy scholarship in the social sciences. This is perhaps not surprising in a situation where, for instance, by 2050 the UK government is aiming to achieve near-zero carbon emissions, and 30% of the country's total energy demand is accounted for by domestic energy consumption. Indeed Gram-Hanssen's study of teenagers and domestic laundry in Denmark was developed in a context where 'around one third of all energy' in Denmark was consumed by households (Gram-Hanssen 2005). In this context there are a number of reasons why ethnographers of the home should be interested in energy, and in why policy makers concerned with the reduction of carbon emissions should likewise be interested in ethnographic understandings of everyday domestic life, across different national contexts. That social scientists might approach understanding domestic energy through the study of practices is well established in the sociological literature. Shove has, through a focus on socio-technical processes, investigated 'how expectations and practices change, at what rate, in what direction, and with what consequence for the consumption of environmentally critical resources like energy and water' (2003: 16); and Gram-Hanssen has accounted for both cultural and socio-technical constructions and 'the individual determinants of understanding the differences in practices' (2008: 3). These sociological approaches have been engaged for understanding energy consumption through laundry practices in the work of Gram-Hanssen (2005) in Denmark as I noted above and, in the UK, Shove (2003) has analysed how 'routine and habit' in laundry practices, with a focus on sustainability. Anthropological approaches also increasingly provide new insights in this field and it is clear that, as Harold Wilhite has put it 'energy needs anthropology' (2005: 1). Anthropologists have in fact, albeit to a limited extent, since the last century, contributed to knowledge on energy technologies, policies and practices through research in, for example, the United States (see Nader 2006, 2010, Wilk n.d.). The anthropological contribution to energy studies is moreover increasingly evident, for instance, in Sweden (Henning 2005, 2006), India (Wilhite 2008), Japan and Norway (Wilhite et al. 1996) and England (Pink 2011d).

To begin understanding everyday life domestic practices and energy use *ethnographically* as part of the sensory home, a first reference point is the existing anthropological literature on the home. Anthropologists of the home have developed sophisticated understandings of domestic consumption. In doing so they have focused on: how residents negotiate with the external agencies of the state, the landlord or previous owners; the constitution of identity; and the materiality and sensoriality of home (e.g. Miller 1988, 1998, 2001, Clarke 2001, Pink 2004). This has included the analysis of housework and laundering (Pink 2004, 2005, 2007d), home decoration (Miller 1988, 2001, Pink 2004), food practices (e.g. Hecht 2001, Petridou 2001, Sutton 2006) and radio use (Tacchi 1998). As Wilhite has pointed out, 'people do not consume energy *per se*, but rather the things energy makes possible, such as light, clean clothes, travel, refrigeration and so on' (Wilhite 2005: 2, original italics, and see Shove 2003). Thus existing ethnographic studies have already indirectly engaged with everyday practices that consume energy. For instance, re-consider listening to the radio (e.g. Tacchi 1998) or cooking (e.g. Sutton 2006) as practices that use energy. In Chapter 4, we saw how a detailed analysis of washing up, which was treated differently in my earlier work (Pink 2004), demonstrated how electricity and/or gas is needed to heat water so that it is sensed to be hot enough to get clean dishes, while the need for and availability of hot water was also contingent on other persons, moralities, technologies and materialities. The existing anthropology of the home, through its emphasis on materiality, agency, self-identity and the senses offers a set of methodological and conceptual tools, adding to what Wilhite notes as the potential already offered by anthropology, 'for example, in understanding the ways in which family relations (kinship), gender, relations of production, meaning and morals are all mutually implicated in the uses of energy' (Wilhite 2005: 2). Yet to study energy involves a novel step: while anthropological studies of the home have tended to focus on material culture (e.g. Miller 2001) and the sensory home (Pink 2004), energy is not material or visible; it is not something we touch, listen to or smell. For instance, while I might suggest sitting on a comfortable sofa, with a warm drink, to watch a film with my family, I would not suggest that we sit together to consume energy. Yet consuming energy would be integral to the constitution of that material, digital, multisensory and social environment.

The analysis of domestic energy consumption through a focus on identifiable practices (as suggested by, for instance, Shove 2003 and Gram-Hanssen 2008) is certainly an important route through which to engage with such an invisible research subject (see Pink 2011d). Here, therefore, I analyse everyday domestic practices as part of a wider process of the constitution of the home as an aesthetic arena. In what follows, first I establish how a phenomenological approach to domestic energy-consuming practices can build on the critical perspectives already developed in the social sciences. I then elaborate on the concept of the sensory home, before suggesting how everyday life practices might be situated through a theory of the home as place. As my discussion of laundry flows reveals, energy consumption is part of the sensory and affective practices of individual practitioners that are integral to the constitution of home-as-place.

ENERGY IN THE SENSORY HOME-PLACE

In existing literature the aesthetic qualities of the 'mundane' practices of everyday domestic life have rarely been acknowledged as a subject for analysis. Yet the need for a concept that acknowledges the experiential is evident in energy studies, where, for example, the notion of 'comfort' is used by social scientists (e.g. Shove 2003, Henning 2006, Gram-Hanssen 2008), and by scholars across disciplines. In my book *Home Truths* (Pink 2004), I have argued that we conceptualise the home as a multisensory environment, and as such attend to how it is both experienced and constituted. My past research demonstrated how a number of activities might participate in the constitution of the sensory home. This includes, for example, housework and home creativity practices that maintain surfaces and objects (e.g. carpets vacuumed, kitchen surfaces and baths cleaned), regulate the olfactory home (e.g. cooking, plug-ins, open windows, burning oils, laundering sheets) and create what people call 'atmosphere' (e.g. burning candles, electric lighting, television, music playing, radio) (see Pink 2004, 2005, 2007d). Many of these practices involve using sources of gas or electricity or have implications for their use (e.g. the temperature changes related to open windows).

The sensory home can therefore be understood as an ecology of interrelated practices, discourses, materiality and energies through which homes and self-identities are continually co-constituted as part of the of home. As we saw in Chapter 4, this is also a social process that involves visitors to the home, and in households with multiple residents it involves the socialities, power relations and intersecting energy use practices and needs of different people, themselves always in movement. If we think of home being a place-event with an intensity of the interrelations of persons, things and sensations, we can understand energy use as an essential part of the making of the home. Energy is consumed in practices that are integral to the movement and renewal of constituents of place. The practices through which it is consumed are negotiated socially, experienced multisensorially and involve both unspoken knowing and conscious awareness of discourses about, for example, temperatures, the environment and morality. Doing the laundry is one of the skilled multisensory practices of everyday domestic life. It involves embodied knowing, sensing, ways of doing that are rarely articulated verbally, but that are essential to the successful accomplishment of its various stages (see Pink 2005, 2007d) and to the constitution of the home as place.

LAUNDRY, MOVEMENT AND THE SENSORY HOME

The opening paragraph to this chapter already describes something of the role of laundry in the constitution of the sensory home. This might include the smell of laundry drying in front of the gas fire in the winter, the noise of the machine, or the visual effects of items hanging over a hot radiator. Laundry is always in process – it is in movement, however slowly, creating routes through the sensory home, changing the sensory constitution and experience of rooms as it moves. When I began to research laundry practices, I had assumed my focus would be on the laundry basket and the machine. Yet I was soon to realise that laundry is not limited to the weekly or daily wash routine, but is also embedded in longer-term domestic cycles which contribute to the shifting constitution of the sensory home. Within this, different items in the same room might have varying trajectories regarding the laundry process. During the interviews and video ethnography, I explored the types of laundry different rooms in the home held to bring this issue to the fore. For example, as we sat in Jane's living room, she described to me the different stages and routes of the laundry items that were part of the room. Below I quote the conversation at length to reveal the complexities of the different routes that laundry from one room might take, and the different energy sources that would be used for this:

Sarah   And I wanted to ask you what you've got in here by way of laundry.

Jane   Ooh right, um, now all the cushion covers come off, that comes off there, um, I've not done these yet, wait a minute. These come off but these have got to be done, the bottom of the cushions … [and would be washed with a laundry detergent product]

Sarah   They are ready are they?

Jane   I think they are ready to be done.

Sarah   How long have they been on there without being done?

Jane   Ooh dear me, six month, pretty bad.

Sarah   Yeah, and what about the cushion covers, how long?

Jane   Em, these, well I do these about once every three months.

Sarah	And how do you actually know when they are ready to be done?
Jane	Uh grubby.
Sarah	They look grubby?
Jane	Yes.
Sarah	But what stage are they at the moment?
Jane	Well, not, not bad, as I say, these we could do with some new ones, but we are in the middle of a DIY phase at the moment, so they will probably be the last to be done.
Sarah	And um, you've got this rabbit on here.
Jane	Oh yes, um, he, well I just like my, with having two boys, I'm deprived of the dolls and the soft toys so that's my idea, I do like my soft toys and um, my teddy …
Sarah	When you wash them do they actually get put in the washing machine?
Jane	No they don't, I sort of like dust them down, Sarah, and I'll sort of vacuum it, vacuum them.
Sarah	The curtains here, these ones you say they go into …
Jane	No, I shall wash those, because as I say they're um, old, and there, we need them changing, so as I say I've got to, that's got to be my next task.

These tasks enabled Jane to maintain a sensory aesthetic balance in her living room – to achieve this she used the washing machine and vacuum and also periodically replaced items. As we continued I found that other practices requiring other sources of energy and cooperation might be needed, as she used hot water to wash the rugs in the bath:

Jane	Um, well, I do like pattern carpets and I sort of, I've got a … [carpet cleaning technology]. But these rugs, as I say this one needs doing again. These, I soak them in [laundry detergent product] in the bath … And I find it fantastic. I do, but it is a chore because my husband has to lift them out when they are full of water, because they are very heavy and they take about two days to dry, but I find the [product] fantastic for sort of fetching them up, Sarah.
Sarah	And how often do you do that?
Jane	Once every six months. But as I say you see they've come through the house, they don't take their shoes off, so they get grubby very quickly.

In Jane's living room we talked about some of the slower moving constituents of the sensory home. However the same principle can be used to understand how faster moving laundry participates in the constitution of the aesthetics of a room. Bed sheets tend to be changed every week or every two weeks, something that, as Angela described it, is part of the sensory home. We were discussing the way she likes her home to smell, and of course laundry is just one component in this:

Angela	[I] Go round with the air freshener. I tend to find, again, that I'm a bit heavy handed, so it gets a bit overpowering, so we use the air freshener then open the windows, just to calm it down a bit but you still get the lingering nice smell. I use [spray-on product]. It doesn't really create a smell, does it, but it does mask any odours that are about … I don't use things on the carpet. I use [product].
Sarah	What do you use the [spray-on product] on then?
Angela	The furniture, mainly the settee, things like that.
Sarah	And what about your laundry, is it important how your laundry smells?
Angela	Yes.
Sarah	What does it have to smell of?
Angela	Fabric conditioner … I love the smell, when you get it out of the washing machine and the smell hits you, the fabric conditioner and I mean, like I said, I changed the girls' beds this morning. Unfolding all my washing, I could smell my fabric, and making my beds I could smell. I think getting into a clean bed, and you can smell the wash powder/fabric conditioner, it's lovely.

Bathroom towels are another good example. During our tour of her home, Alice and I entered the bathroom, prompting our discussion of the towels:

Sarah	Mm-mm. And what do you do about the towels and bath mat and all those sorts of things? Does everyone have a shower or bath every day?
Alice	Yes … The bath mat I tend to put on the line, and the towel goes in the linen basket.
Sarah	Do you just have one towel for everybody in the morning?
Alice	Yes, in general, yes.
Sarah	And then that's washed every day, is it?
Alice	Well, not every day, but it is changed every day. I'll do it when I've got a load.
Sarah	So the last person who gets it when it's a bit soggy doesn't complain then?
Alice	No. Well, actually it's usually [daughter 1] and myself because [daughter 2] has her own towels.
Sarah	Right. And your husband does … ?
Alice	He'll grab whatever's there. He'll generally … um … he has a wash in the morning and he has a bath at night, so when he's finished it can come out quite dirty sometimes.

Towels are one of the most prominent items of domestic laundry in terms of their visibility and daily use. There are a number of ways that they participate in the constitution and the experience of the sensory home. Moreover, towels are not just for the bathroom, as hand towels, kitchen towels, swimming pool towels and dog towels also figure. Participants often discussed how towels change in texture from fluffy to soggy, stiff or rough (see also Pink 2005). Towels may also move from the bathroom towel rail to the side of the bath, be thrown on the floor, end up crumpled up on top of the radiator or be put in the laundry basket or in the machine. Towels also need to be dried and this often requires an energy source as they might be equally pegged out outdoors, hung on a drying rack, placed on or near radiators or a heater, or put in an airing cupboard or in the tumble dryer. Research participants each described their preferences for these different drying options in terms of the textures they produced (for example, a tumble drier might make towels fluffier while drying them over a radiator could make them feel like cardboard).

Our discussions of laundry items as they were encountered through the different rooms of each home brought to the fore the roles they play in the making and maintaining of the constantly shifting sensory aesthetics of the home. Moreover, while we might associate particular items with particular types of room, it is important to realise that obvious domestic laundry items – like towels, sheets and clothing – are not static. Yet neither are items we might not usually think of as laundry – such as curtains and rugs. They are all part of the process of continual movement, making a meshwork (Ingold 2008) of the traces of things as they move around and in and out of the home. These movements, if carried out to precision – or near enough, ensure that the home maintains a series of aesthetic qualities through which it is perceived as a home. That is, they constitute it as a sensory home-place through their movement. These qualities may be sensed in relation to discourses on cleanliness and morality. Yet the extent to which different individuals ascribe to and live up to culturally specific notions of and ways of defining clean and dirty may be negotiated in relation to a series of identity factors (see Pink 2005) and might be contingent on specific circumstances. This means that collective standards and moral discourses are recognised but not always embedded in practices as they are lived out behind closed doors when others cannot see, or do not know. For example, Angela, who would normally hide her pending ironing in her bedroom when a friend was coming over, described an 'awful' experience:

> The other week, I got all my washing, and what I did, I sorted it out into piles and spread it all round the kitchen, and I thought, I can't be bothered to do this, so I actually sat down on the settee, and I was reading a brilliant book at the time, so I sat down, read the book and somebody knocked on the door I'd not seen for about 10–12 months … 'cos she was a work colleague as well – and she'd just left to have a baby … She came round to show me the baby and see the house because she's not seen the house – it was horr… – it was – I cringe at the thought of it.

Therefore Angela's laundry had taken an unconventional route, and had found a temporary stopping place that 'upset' the moral aesthetics of the home as she felt it should be when presented to others. The particular configuration of home where conventions and the performance of a practice had become dislocated became problematic. This can be seen as another example of how the performance of practices might sustain or disrupt a desired domestic aesthetic during the course of 'normal' everyday life. Angela had changed her conventional laundry route by taking some time to relax. As such she performed the practice of doing the laundry in an innovative way to allow for another experience of the home. Yet the experience of this practice was socially contingent in that once her colleague arrived to visit, the domestic aesthetic it created felt 'wrong', putting the sensory affective home and self into disarray. Unconventional laundry routes were also represented in the work of Gram-Hanssen in Denmark, although in a rather different way. She comments in her qualitative interviews about teenager laundry, that 'several parents described that in their opinion teenagers sometimes, or very often, put clothes to be washed, just because it was easier than folding them and return them to their place. So if clothes had left the wardrobe, the only way back was through the washing machine, even when the clothes had not been worn, but just came out together with something else or because the teenager was considering whether to wear it' (Gram-Hanssen 2005). This example suggests that conventional and innovative practices can simultaneously be engaged in the constitution of the sensory home. A 'proper' laundry route was appropriated by teenagers and used for clean clothing, and parents incorporated these out-of-place laundry items into a conventional process; thus maintaining the aesthetic balance of the home.

LAUNDRY LINES AND THE 'MESHWORK' OF HOME

The examples discussed in the previous section show that laundry items are continually circulating around the home. They travel at different speeds and in different ways, their sensory qualities are transformed as they move, and by following them around the home we can understand how energy consumption is intertwined with the ways people use them, their movement and renewal. In this section I consider how some of the faster moving laundry items – such as clothing, towels and sheets – participate in the process of the home, through the idea of 'laundry lines'. The notion of lines reflects Ingold's (2007, 2008) notion of place as a 'meshwork' discussed in Chapter 2. Laundry lines are negotiated in relation to the nature of the laundry item being dealt with, the energy sources that are implicated in both its soiling and its renewal, social relations and moralities. With each research participant we (re)enacted a 'normal' laundry process from the stage of collecting the laundry from the place it is usually deposited (the laundry basket) to pegging it outside or elsewhere to dry. We also discussed questions relating to how the laundry arrived in the basket and where it would be stored, ironed or otherwise processed afterwards. Laundry does not necessarily begin in the laundry basket, but is an ongoing process. Participants described to me how and where they 'found' the laundry items distributed by different family members, in bedrooms, on the floor. They also discussed the measures that had to be taken to procure dirty items of clothing that other family members still wanted to wear, and strategies for returning items to the places where they would be found if clean, if they disagreed with the dirty classification allocated to them by other family members. These can all be seen as ways of limiting the extent to which these laundry items disrupt the sensory aesthetic of home as they are sensed as both dirty and out of place.

Thus the practice of doing laundry can be seen to both follow and constitute lines through the home. From the basket, if one is used, to the machine, a 'bunch' of laundry is transported, sometimes sorted into whites and colours and according to the type of wash it should be subjected to. The laundry goes into the machine, with decisions made regarding temperatures (sometimes this means just always leaving it on the same cycle and at other times it is constantly changing), and while it is being washed there is usually an opportunity to engage in another task. Once the laundry is taken out, it is evaluated in a way that is multisensory. Participants used modern Western categories to discuss with me how the visual, tactile and olfactory experiences of sorting or pegging out newly washed laundry informed their decisions and definitions of it. The routes laundry items take from the machine vary depending on the sensory qualities that practitioners aim to achieve as well as the configurations in which they are operating. For instance, they might go to a tumble dryer, to a clothes horse in front of a heating source, or be draped over a radiator. Once dry they may be returned to their previous location, put away, kept aside before ironing or ironed straight away. Ironing might be done while watching television. Not everyone irons however, and not everything is ironed.

It is important to remember though that when laundry is moved through a home it is *not* moving *in* the home, but it is moving as part of the home, and in relation to the other things that make up home. Laundry is part of the ecology of things that make the textures, smells and visual appearance of home and the affective affordances of home and it is embedded in the socialities of home. Laundry practices therefore are integral to the constitution of the sensory home. The laundry lines that these practices are interwoven with thus participate in the making of home as place-event. To understand how energy is used in the home, therefore, it is instructive to follow the routes that domestic practices forge in their moving through and creating environments. As I have indicated above, a range of primary and secondary uses of gas and electricity are implicated in doing the laundry. In the next section I focus on how tumble dryers and radiators are implicated in routes through the home to explore how social and environmental elements are involved in the making of laundry lines and the implications of this for energy consumption.

DOMESTIC SOCIALITIES, AESTHETICS AND TECHNOLOGIES

Existing research has emphasised the social relations of laundry. For instance, Kaufmann's interview-based study undertaken in France focused on the couple (Kaufmann 1998). An interrogation of Kaufmann's examples begins to suggest how the stopping places and routes taken by laundry and technology are interwoven with the gendered relationships of French couples. For example, he discusses how in one household the husband would leave his clothes in a pile because he was not sure if they needed to be washed. This, Kaufmann points out, meant that they were 'not in their proper place' and would be moved by the wife (1998: 92). In another example, the wife would often hang out the laundry when she and her husband were just about to go out and Kaufmann tells us 'their relationship became highly fraught', motivating them to buy a tumble dryer (1998: 179). Similarly Gram-Hanssen's work with teenagers and laundry in Denmark, noted above, demonstrates the relevance of generational differences to the production of laundry (Gram-Hanssen 2005). The significance of the social relations of laundry practices and flows is likewise demonstrated well through my UK laundry ethnography. Yet the nature of these materials brings a further theme to the fore by suggesting how such relationships are embedded in spatial, material and technological relations. Below I develop the discussion by reflecting on how participants described their relationships with husbands, tumble dryers and radiators, and the aesthetics of the everyday routes they were not prepared to create through their homes.

Drying laundry when it was raining was an issue for the participants. Angela's husband could not bear to have laundry drying on radiators around the house, so she only did this when he was out. Otherwise she would wait for a fine day before washing rather than use her tumble dryer. She explained to me that:

Angela I have got a tumble dryer … but – I don't know whether the heating element has gone on it – it will only work when it's on low heat … And – so – and plus I've not got power in the garage … So I've then got to run an extension from my bedroom into the garage and everything else and it's just too much bother. It keeps cutting – when you put it on high heat – and I think that the low heat is not worth having it on … I mean – I've managed alright without it … Um – I've got one of these clothes airers as well. He actually bought me that as our first Christmas present.

As she went on to say, both the location of the dryer and the cost informed her practices:

Angela I think if it was sort of like – here – it would get used a lot … Again it's the cost point of view as well – they are meant to be very expensive to run – so I can manage without it.
Sarah Is cost a real issue?
Angela Yeah … I'd rather have sort of like £5.00 extra in my pocket than £5.00 on the electricity bill.

Yet, if necessary, she would be prepared to use other energy sources:

Angela If I was really in need or – or I would go to the launderette … I don't think I'd ever get really in need. Um – I mean if I was struggling I'd put the central heating on and things would go on the radiator.

Jane, who had some items drying on radiators as we toured her home, likewise preferred not to use radiator heat, or a tumble dryer:

Sarah Do you find you have to use your radiators a lot in the winter?
Jane Eh, I don't Sarah because it makes it too, it makes it all stiff. I'd sooner them go on the clothes horse and dry naturally I would, because as I say, I did have a tumble dryer but em, as I say at the moment, my husband will get me another one Sarah, but he wants to put it in the shed. Now I won't have it cos I'm not traipsing …
        …
Jane Um, now if I have a tumble dryer I want it in here because I'm not traipsing down that shed with wet washing on a wet day, no thank you! I'd sooner put in on my, in winter I don't want it, so um, when we have a little bit of a flip round, I may, I may let him get me one Sarah, as I say, but I don't, the tumble dryers I don't consider them a necessity.

Sarah	Is that partly because of the way you use the breakfast bar at the moment then, would you have to give that up if you have a tumble dryer?
Jane	Well, well we'd have to get, we'd have to lose sort of one seat, my hostess trolley I only use sort of a couple of times, that'll move in there, one of these seats will go there, so I may have room for one Sarah but as I say, one will have to come up at the right price because we're not going to spend a fortune on one, we're not.

Laundry lines are therefore part of the whole experience of moving through and around the home. They are related to perceptions of indoors and outdoors, contingent on the weather, on social relationships in the home and on existing spatial arrangements. They also clearly delineate what these participants understand as the home and the outside (the garage and the shed). These understandings, which inform how people move around in and live in the sensory home, also influence the way their everyday practices involve energy consumption. Thus the sensory aesthetics of home are also made *because of* the way laundry lines are deliberately created or navigated in relation to the weather, husbands, dryers, radiators and more. The participants knew how to move in their homes so that their sensory experience of home would in itself be more satisfactory. In terms of the consumption of energy, laundry lines directly connect to energy-consuming devices – for instance, most obviously, the hot water supplies in the bathroom, the washing machine itself, the iron and perhaps the tumble dryer. Yet laundry lines may also appropriate existing technologies, such as whole central heating systems, radiators and gas fires. They moreover are designed to avoid the experience of a domestic aesthetic or route that is unappealing – the rush to the shed or running cables to the garage in the rain. These navigations through the 'weather world' (Ingold 2010b) are also implicated in energy use.

The routes that laundry practices follow can thus be seen as navigations through and simultaneously productive of a multisensory environment. In this process energy-consuming technologies and their spatial arrangement both structure how routes are chosen, and are appropriated as launderers seek alternative, innovative or less obvious routes to achieving the most satisfactory multisensory transformations of their laundry.

LAUNDRY, EXPERIENTIAL KNOWING AND DISCOURSES OF ENERGY

The analysis above has shown how the contingencies of energy consumption are inextricable from the sensory, material, social and environmental

processes of home. Before concluding, however, I reflect on how participants articulated these domestic activities in relation to energy use.

The precise ways people do the laundry can depend on the times of
the day they are at home to carry out tasks – putting on the machine,
pegging out in the garden, hanging laundry near or on radiators, the
times they get up and go to work, and the material structure of the
home. These different elements converge in specific ways and indeed
people might reflect on this to explain how and when energy is used or
'saved'. For example, Angela described how because it was impossible to
reach the plug socket for her washing machine to install a timer on it,
she had to depend on her husband switching it on before going to work
in order to benefit from cheaper electricity. Thus showing how energy
was consumed was determined by this configuration of social, technological, spatial and routine elements.

The prospect of saving money through consuming less energy can
also be seen as part of the negotiation of priorities. As she examined
some of her laundry, Alice and I discussed what it was she liked better
about laundry that had been dried outside. She told me:

Alice   This sounds stupid, but you know when you go for a nice walk,
         and the winds blowing through and you just feel fresh. I just
         think the washing smells like that when it's been outside, and I
         think the white clothes as well … I think the sun tends to bleach
         them a little and make them white.
Sarah   … you were saying you liked the smell of the fabric conditioner?
Alice   Yes I do. I just like to put them out. And of course it doesn't cost
         you anything to put them outside, does it?
Sarah   I mean, what about the texture of them, do they actually feel
         different when they're dried outside as well or not?
Alice   In the winter when I dry clothes – sometimes I put them on
         the clothes airer; if they've not been in the tumble dryer they're
         harder. When you put them out they are quite soft. They're quite
         soft when you put them in the tumble dryer as well actually if you
         just spin them round for 10 minutes or so. It reduces the ironing
         as well … Not cotton things in particular; but if you put things
         like nylon or this kind of thing. This is actually cotton but I don't
         mean cotton like T-shirts, you know, crisp. Socks and underwear
         and things like that, nightwear especially, if you … when I bring
         them in off the line and put them in the tumble dryer just for sort
         of 10 minutes, I sort of fold them up straight away and that's it …

Here, the importance of the sensory aesthetic of the home and the laundry from which it is composed therefore comes through strongly as a
way of understanding why energy is used. The tumble dryer was important for achieving the sensory experiences desired from laundry.

With Helen, I also discussed the merits of pegging out and tumble dryers. When we were discussing whether Helen (who commented that she thought she should think a bit more about the environment) liked pegging out, she told me:

Helen   No, I mean it depends, it's just … I don't like it when there's a load and it's loads of little socks, and bibs and things like that and it takes ages. But no, it just … and it's quite satisfying then to come in and see it all blowing on the line and … No, I don't mind that.

Sarah   Is that when you feel satisfied then?

Helen   Yeah. When I'm standing in my kitchen washing my dishes and I've … yes. Sometimes I … have been known to put the tumble dryer on even when I could take it out simply because while I've probably got the ironing board up and [son]'s having a long sleep, if I can get that load dried and I can quickly get it ironed, whereas if I've got to put it on the line and wait for it to dry longer, then it will have to wait till the next time I put the ironing board up.

Sarah   So why don't you tell [husband] that you do that?

Helen   I don't know really because he doesn't shout … he's not one of these husbands who says 'You can't use your tumble dryer between May and September' at all. He wouldn't know if I'd used it or not.

Sarah   Do you feel guilty then about using the electricity very much?

Helen   No. People have got all their lines of washing blowing on the line and I'm using the tumble dryer. I feel naughty.

Like other participants, for Helen, as an individual practitioner, everyday decisions although taken quickly, drew on complex sets of material, sensory and social knowledge. Putting the ironing board up or down, having laundry flows disrupted because they are not ready for the next stage, and pegging out or not, are also processes through which the sensory and affective home-place is constituted.

As these three examples reveal, when people do consider questions about energy use, they may weigh this up against other factors relating to the possibilities that they have to navigate their sensory homes in terms of existing structures, relationships and other practices and to ways that they can ensure that an appropriate aesthetic balance is maintained.

SUSTAINABILITY, ENERGY AND THE ENTANGLEMENTS OF HOME

In this chapter my analysis has focused on how movement, materiality, the senses, sociality, technology and the weather are implicated in the way the everyday practice of doing the laundry is performed. In doing so I have shown how laundry practices are implicated in the complex process of the constitution of the sensory home, and subsequently in the contingencies of the ways in which energy is consumed. As we have seen, laundry practices have elements that are routine and that are contingent; they entail innovations that are designed to navigate and negotiate with the various other agencies and processes of home. Putting this in the theoretical terms introduced in Chapter 2, therefore, we can see how laundry practices are interwoven in the constitution of home, and that moreover to understand their performance one needs to account for their relationality with other practices, processes, things and persons. To understand this process, the idea of the flow of everyday life becomes not a methodological 'problem' but rather a route to follow. As laundry flows and moves with people through the home, it becomes implicated in the entanglement of home as place as it both contributes to the sensory aesthetic of the home and is shaped by the other components. Methodologically, therefore, I have shown how by acknowledging the centrality of flow and of actual movement to domestic life and following the laundry and the participants as they move through the sensory home, we might develop some new insights into how home is experienced and constituted, and into how everyday performances of laundry practices become implicated in the consumption of domestic energy.

The analysis has shown commonalities in the social, material and environmental intersections that led participants to innovate, rearrange routes and appropriate technologies. This included the spatial layout of the home and appliances, relationships and negotiations with other household members, the need to create particular forms of sensory experience through the transformation of laundry items, and the weather. Likewise we should acknowledge that laundry practices, as for any other practice, are also interwoven with other practices of everyday life, and further exploration of these relations will also bring new knowledge to the fore. As the analysis here has shown, the intersections between different processes of place through which home is constituted do not necessarily lead to the same ways of using washing machines, dryers, sunlight, radiators or gas fires and other energy-using appliances as part of the laundry process. Yet they illustrate how analytically we might identify a series of intersections that become prisms through which differences might be viewed.

CONCLUSION

In Chapter 4, I focused on the detail of practice as part of the constitution of home through a comparison of two individuals. In this chapter I have brought together the experiences of five women living in rather similar situations. My aim has not been to make an empirical point through this small sample about how energy is used in British homes. Rather, my argument is that this approach, which takes the constitution of the sensory home as its analytical starting point and follows the lines through which this place is made, offers a new route to scholarly and applied knowledge about how and why energy is consumed in the home.

From the starting point of understanding the sensory home as place, we can begin to understand how practices – as things that are performed *as part of* rather than *done to* the home – are implicated in the making of a domestic sensory aesthetic. By following the persons and things that are integral to particular practices as they move through the home, we are able to gain an understanding of the relationships between these activities and the environment. Laundry practices offer an interesting illustration because the movement of persons and things is obvious and visible, as are the material and sensory transformations involved.

6

TRACING NEIGHBOURHOOD FLOWS: MAKING A GARDEN PLACE

In the summer of 2007, at the end of a video tour of the Green Lanes Community Garden, I asked David, the chairman of the garden committee and one of the main gardeners involved in the project, how he felt when he stood and looked at the garden. He told me:

> Proud I suppose, that's nice to see flowers as opposed to just a bit of field, and of course that was just a muddy field wasn't it, no one walked down into town across here, on a wet day.

Since its formation in 2005, the Green Lanes Community Garden project in Aylsham, Norfolk (UK) has transformed a piece of suburban wasteland into a beautiful garden filled with the colour and scent of flowers, grass lawns, benches and not least pathways (Figures 6.1 and 6.2). The land initially referred to as the 'field' when I first started my ethnographic research in the town in 2005, and later as a 'garden', is surrounded by suburban houses and bungalows whose private gardens back onto its land to form something of an uneven rectangle marked by high wooden fences, painted green, on one side and a wire surround on the other.

I was told that before the inception of the project, there had been a number of concerns about the 'field', an ex-playground site, which was unkempt and prone, some feared, to vandalism, or could even have had a block of flats built on it. As Andrew, the project's fundraiser, put it: 'It fell into disrepair and it was just a nothing piece of ground, a bit of an eyesore, just used for dogs running and messing.' Its long grass, when wet, deemed it impassable as a shortcut to the town centre. This, David stressed (and as was mentioned at a committee meeting I attended), made the elderly and young mums with pushchairs take a longer route

Figure 6.1   From field ... © Sarah Pink

Figure 6.2   ... to garden © Sarah Pink, with thanks to Aylsham Town
Council Archive

around the local roads. The project to develop the field was supported
by the town council (to whom the land belonged) and a local charity
(the Aylsham Care Trust [ACT]). It was also congruent with the aims of
the international Cittaslow (Slow City) movement of which Aylsham is
a member town and was thus part of the town's Cittaslow programme
and identity. The development and management of the garden was undertaken by a group of local resident volunteers, including a fundraiser,

people responsible for publicity and the gardeners themselves. The tour of the garden cited above was the last in a series of video tours of the garden I shared with David (and sometimes his wife Anne) at intervals of a few months between the summers of 2005 and 2007 during my return visits to Aylsham within a wider multi-sited ethnographic research project about Cittaslow and sustainability in towns in the UK. David and Anne were my main sources on the development of the garden, and with whom I developed walking tours. Yet this was part of a mixed ethnographic approach in which I also met other residents – some in the garden itself – attended a committee meeting and steering group meeting and participated in other events and met with others connected with the project.

In this chapter I continue the focus on practice and place through an analysis of how local residents' engagements with this uneven rectangle of land make evident the intersections between local ways of knowing, socialities, local government processes, global commercial processes and transnational activist agendas. The Green Lanes Community Garden is a particularly suitable example for this exercise. The story of the garden unfolds in the suburban neighbourhood of a small English town in a rural agricultural region, with a total population of about 6,000 people. Yet, through its involvement with Cittaslow and the fundraising practices of its committee members, the garden is implicated in complex and sometimes seemingly contradictory ways with global commercial and activist processes.

At first glance the community garden project appears to be a local concern: a committee of local residents manages it with the support of ACT and the town council. Its planning stage was supported by the Widening Adult Participation Action Fund (WAPAF) and the Learning Skills Council (LSC). Later it had financial support from the Norfolk Rural Community Council and the local Rotary club and a local nursery donated unwanted plants. Moreover, the embodied labour of digging, planting, adding a section of turf and tending the garden, as well as the planning, funding applications and contracting of builders to create pathways – all provided by a series of local residents – have been essential to its production. However, once one starts to unpick the flows that intersect in the production, identity and maintenance of the garden, it emerges as an example of how everyday embodied practices are bound up with global processes. Indeed this is a common feature of community gardens, apparently particularly in recent years. For example, Ferris et al. note that 'Although community gardens do have a long history there is no doubt that they have been given a fresh impetus by the emergence of international concern with the environment and sustainability. Local Agenda 21, agreed at the UN Conference on the Environment held in

Rio de Janeiro in June 1992, placed great emphasis on sustainable development at the local level' (2001: 562). The most obvious international framing of the Green Lanes community garden is that it is part of a Cittaslow town. In common with Ferris et al.'s (2001) point, Local Agenda 21 was one of the drivers in the establishment of Cittaslow UK in 2004, and is part of its membership criteria. Moreover, the fundraising for the garden has gone beyond seeking support from local businesses and public organisations and some of the garden's facilities have been provided through funds that have been successfully applied for from larger entities such as a big supermarket chain and a bank.

INTRODUCTION

Everyday-life scholars have long since been interested in the notion of neighbourhood. Pierre Mayol, who worked with de Certeau on the practice of everyday life, undertook a study of a neighbourhood of Lyon in France. Mayol was concerned with the tactics of the neighbourhood. Most relevant for the discussion in this chapter, he suggested that the anonymous public space of the neighbourhood becomes colonised by 'a *private particularized space* [which] insinuates itself as a result of the practical everyday use of this space' (1998: 9, original italics). Thus practices of neighbourhood involve 'a sort of appropriation' of public space (1998: 11). Mayol, moreover, defines the neighbourhood as a locality that is experienced by walking. He suggests it is 'a domain in which the space-time relationship is the most favourable for a dweller who moves from place to place *on foot, starting from his or her home*'; in short, 'it is the result of a *walk*' (1998: 10, original italics). Both of these themes form part of the discussion below, although following the approach to practice and place outlined in Chapter 2, my treatment of them is developed in new ways.

In this chapter I approach neighbourhood practices and place through an analysis of the community garden. In doing so I extend the theoretical discussion to explore how localities might be understood in relation to global flows. I also introduce an examination of how place and practice shift over time by analysing how this specific locality was transformed through the activities of local residents over two years, between 2005 and 2007. The analysis continues the theme of sustainability established in Chapters 4 and 5, now through an exploration of how the convergence of a particular set of practices creates and maintains the constantly changing but sustainable garden with a locally meaningful aesthetic. Therefore the task of this chapter requires a framework for conceptualising the everyday human and material relationships and embodied knowing of 'local' everyday suburban life in relation to global processes. To understand the nature of these connections demands an appreciation of both the phenomenology and politics of place, and an understanding of how practice is implicated in the constitution of place. Here I extend the interdisciplinary intersections outlined in Chapter 2 to explore how ethnographic and theoretical insights might contribute to understanding the relationships between the global flows implied by transnational activism, on the one hand, and everyday experiences as fleeting as encountering the scent of a flower as one walks through a public garden, on the other.

In Chapter 5 I discussed an approach to researching 'invisible' energy used in the home, similarly in this chapter I seek to understand what is not directly evident: how a 'local' suburban neighbourhood is connected to global flows in ways that are not immediately visible. Again, extending the analysis to a different context, building on the notion of the sensory home which informed the discussions of Chapters 4 and 5, in this chapter I attend to the making of a garden as the production of a certain sensory aesthetic.

Community gardens are widespread internationally and offer an interesting example of how places might be constituted and lived. A good number of academic studies have been developed in the United States, where, even in 2001, Hilda Kurtz wrote that already there had been a 'remarkable proliferation of community gardens on vacant lots in US cities' (2001: 656). There is indeed a broad literature on community gardens internationally, in addition to the US examples, recently spanning, for example, garden projects in Johannesburg in South Africa (Wills et al. 2010), Toronto in Canada (Baker 2004, Wakefield et al. 2007) and Bangkok in Thailand (Fraser 2002). Yet as Kurtz also emphasises, it is important to recognise that community gardens are 'locally differentiated' (2001: 657). Moreover, to my knowledge, most examples discussed in existing literatures tend to be of garden projects developed in cities rather than in smaller urban settlements such as towns. Another tendency in existing work is a focus on the interconnectedness of community gardens within local or regional systems rather than internationally. In contrast, the example outlined here is of a community garden created in a town, yet in the context of its international as well as more local situatedness.

The community garden I discuss here was developed by a committee of residents supported by ACT (the local charity) in a housing area that backed onto a piece of disused land. In this sense its production and use is related primarily to the experience of their immediate environment, local relationships and everyday practices. However, because the garden is part of Aylsham, a member town of Cittaslow, it is also implicated in a wider sustainability agenda, and indeed conforms to the movement's principles. Cittaslow is broadly committed to improving the quality of urban life through a set of principles relating to environmental policy, the local production and consumption of foods, and creating points of contact between consumers and producers, hospitality and increasing awareness of Cittaslow in the towns (outlined in the Cittaslow International Charter: 20–1, http://www.cittaslow.net/immagini/news/statutoEN.pdf). Cittaslow operates through a form of indirect activism that works by creating alternatives to those presented by some types of globalisation (Pink 2009a), thus presenting liveable and experiential examples to local people. Wendy Parkins and Geoffrey Craig have suggested that 'Città Slow represents not a refusal of contemporary global life but an active and critical interrogation of its values, practices and ideologies and provides a site where agency can be exercised in the face of the "inevitabilities" of global culture' (2006: 83). The garden project is indeed exemplary of the type of activity that is used to confirm a town's Cittaslow character and is one of the projects that the movement's local leaders identify as pertaining to Cittaslow. There is also another connection between the garden and Cittaslow principles. Gardening has already been understood through anthropological foci on experience, the senses (e.g. Tilley 2006) and perception (Degnen 2009). Moreover, Parkins and Craig argue that a kind of 'mindful consciousness' that they understand as 'central to slow living generates an awareness of the specificity of place', 'a material relation to the land' and 'an attentiveness to those who co-exist in the same territory and who collectively give their territory value and identity' (2006: 85).

UNDERSTANDING GARDENS

People's relationships with gardens and gardening are complex and, as Catherine Degnen reminds us, 'gardening is by no means a homogeneous practice. It is carried out in multiple sites and by many different practitioners' (2009: 155). It is not my intention to generalise about gardens or gardening and my substantive concern is not with community gardens or gardening per se. Yet the increasing academic literature in this area provides a further context through which to critically situate the discussion. Ferris et al. (2001) suggest that community and private gardens differ in that a community garden is 'in some sense a public garden in terms of ownership, access, and degree of democratic control'. They do not, however, see this as a homogeneous category, pointing out that 'Community gardens exist in many nations and in both urban and rural areas. They vary in what they offer according to local needs. Some

provide open space and greenery. Sometimes they provide cheap veg-
etables for a local community' (Ferris et al. 2001: 560). The Green Lanes
project can be seen as a 'green space', and akin to what Ferris et al. call
a 'pocket park' (2001: 566). As such it can be seen to fall into this broad
category. The Green Lanes community garden can also be seen to share
narratives with the types of community garden described by Troy
Glover, who has reviewed existing literature in this area and stresses
the 'collective' aspects of community gardens. Glover gives primacy
to the *social* networks community gardens imply, suggesting that: 'The
participants' willingness to share resources is only enhanced by the social
connections they make during their participation.' Thus Glover argues
that 'community gardens are less about gardening than they are about
community' and thus should be recognised as contexts for the production
of 'social capital' (2004: 143). Using this framework to analyse a narrative
inquiry with community garden, participants undertaken in a mid-sized
US city, Glover concludes that in this case the community garden' was
a symbol of collective achievement within the neighborhood, the process that led to its development was associated with unequal access to
social capital' (2004: 159).

Glover identifies some key strands in community garden narratives.
The social relations of gardening are indeed important. Yet an emphasis on the social is limiting. As Ash Amin has pointed out with reference more generally to developing an understanding of urban public
space, the focus needs to be shifted to 'the entanglement between
people and the material and visual culture of public space, rather than
solely in the quality of social interaction between strangers'. Thus he
argues that 'the formative sites of urban public culture – collective
forms of being human through shared practices – need not be
restricted to those with a purely human/inter-human character, but
should also include other inputs such as space, technological interme-
diaries, objects, nature and so on' (2008: 8). By suggesting we recognise
the 'entanglement' (a term also used by Ingold [e.g. 2008]) of the
human and non-human, Amin identifies public space as a rather more
complex ecology that cannot be fully comprehended if we privilege
the social. This point is equally applicable to contexts such as community gardens. Indeed, as recent work on gardening demonstrates, an
analysis of the 'relations between people and plants' (Degnen 2009:
152) is called for rather than simply one of garden socialities. In fact,
the notion of *community* garden socialities as an analytical category
might itself be problematised. As I have argued elsewhere, and with
specific reference to this particular garden project (Pink 2008b), the
concept of 'community' is not useful as an analytical category. Indeed
it would seem that the term has been appropriated by those involved

in 'community garden studies' to refer to a particular set of practices, materialities, socialities and ideologies. In this book my use of the term 'community garden' is restricted to refer to a local category, which in this case refers to the experienced garden and the specific embodied practices, socialities and meanings that it involves.

Rather than understanding the garden project as creating a community, a process that is primarily about local sociality, or something that should mainly be understood in terms of the relationship between people and plants, here I define it as a rather more complex intersection or intensity of relations. To understand how it is constituted and indeed is productive of/partly produced by everyday practices, socialities and human–plant interrelations, the garden needs to be understood as equally constituted through global flows, local politics and more. The implication of this shift in focus is that through a theory of place we might enable an analysis that appreciates the complexity of the entanglements that community gardens are. In the next section I first outline a theoretical framework for understanding the intersections between these diverse flows and practices and then discuss the process in more ethnographic detail.

THE COMMUNITY GARDEN AS PLACE

In Chapter 2, I proposed an approach that allows us to understand how human perception, embodied sensory practices and local and global flows are co-implicated in the constitution of place. This approach is particularly suitable for understanding the Green Lanes Community Garden project, but, as I will suggest, is also more generally applicable as a way of understanding the initially invisible relationships between everyday local practice and understandings of locality, activist discourses and global businesses.

In considering the details of processes through which places are constituted in relation to specific localities, anthropological analyses (most notably Feld and Basso 1996, Gupta and Ferguson 1997, Low and Lawrence-Zúñiga 2003, Coleman and Collins 2006) present a wide range of examples. There is an enduring concern in this literature with the relevance of the anthropology of place for understanding the political processes and power relations that are involved. This perspective is particularly pertinent to understanding the community garden within the context of activism and flows related to global businesses. Here I recontextualise this focus with an appreciation of place as developed in Chapter 2. Thus, in the case of the community garden, it would be easy to make the assumption that the garden is a place, bounded by its painted green fence, *in which* people meet and garden and where plants grow, and which moreover a researcher might *go to*, to do ethnography. But by making such an assumption, one would be assigning a set of qualities to the garden as a place, defining it as having set boundaries, and locating a set of things and practices (that might be subjected to an analysis) *in* that place. In the opening passages to this chapter, I indeed identified the garden as a circumscribed piece of land. On one level seeing it as a locality in this sense is useful, in that it gives us a focus, a 'what' and a 'where' to comprehend or look up on Google Earth. But on an analytical level such snapshots are less helpful: in order to understand the garden as a *process* that research participants associated with a material locality, a theory of place that accounts for the multiple movements, flows, agencies and transformations that constitute it is required.

In the previous chapters I have stressed the importance of attending to movement for understanding he constitution of place. Here, likewise, when I started to research the garden project I realised that central to it was the path, at that time just a line tread into the grass, running through it. As time went on I was increasingly aware that the way the garden was experienced and imagined by local people was related both to this route through it and to the movement of plants and persons (Pink 2007e, 2008b). Challenging dominant assumptions that 'we can only live, and know, *in* places' (2008: 1808), Ingold argues that 'to be … is not to be *in* place but to be *along* paths'. For him, 'the path, not the place, is the primary condition of being, or rather of becoming' (2008: 1808, original italics). Thus he has proposed that 'places are formed through movement', they are not 'bound' and indeed 'There could be no places were it not for the comings and goings of human beings and other organisms to and from them, from and to places elsewhere' (2008: 1808). Following this approach then rather than thinking of places as bounded, places that one can *go to* and *be in,* the concept of a 'zone of entanglement' or 'meshwork of interwoven lines' where 'there are no insides or outsides, only openings and ways through' (Ingold 2007: 103) offers an alternative way of conceptualising the garden as a place. However Ingold does not offer an explicit rendering of how such unbounded places might be related to global environmentalist discourses and ideologies, activist projects and flows of capital. One could infer from his analysis that such flows would be part of a 'zone of entanglement' (Ingold 2007) that constitutes place; they might originate in other intensities of entangled trajectories that form part of the wider 'meshwork' that human movement is also part of. Yet from the perspective of how a locality is experienced, and particularly in the instance of the question posed in this chapter, one might want to differentiate between flows that are associated with the local and those that are associated with global or distant sources. For such an analysis, a distinction between space and place becomes useful in that it allows us to conceptualise the way a locality is experienced in terms of a relationship between a set of analytical (albeit constructed) categories – the local, the global and the political. For this purpose, Massey's rendering of the relationship between space and place offers a way of understanding how diverse flows and movements become intertwined in what she calls the 'event of place' (2005: 140–1). Massey understands space as 'open' and 'plural'. Seeing space as 'a simultaneity of stories-so-far', for Massey 'places are collections of these stories, articulations of the wider power-geometries of space' (2005: 130). Thus it is possible to think of places as collections of, or intensities of the interactions between, diverse, plural flows. But Massey argues that we should not assume that place is coherent, that it has 'community or collective identity'. She reminds us rather of the politics of place in that places: 'implicate us, perforce, in the lives of human others, and in our relations with non-humans they ask how we shall respond to our temporary meeting up with these particular rocks and stones and trees' (Massey 2005: 141). As such the community garden project simultaneously offers an example of how place might be constituted through intersections or 'entanglements' (Ingold 2008) that cannot simply be situated through an analysis of the social relations or interactions (Amin 2008) that are implicated in a politics of space (Massey 2005).

In what follows I first focus on the phenomenology of the garden, its materiality and the ways it is known, felt and made. I then examine the global flows whose invisible traces are unavoidably entangled in its intensity.

THE GARDEN(ING)

SENSORY WAYS OF KNOWING IN THE GARDEN

There is an increasing interdisciplinary interest in the concept of 'knowing' (e.g. Wenger 1998). This focuses largely on knowing being inextricable from practical activity, and as being in movement, as Mark Harris has put it:

> … knowing is always bound up in one way or another with the world: a person does not leave their environment to know, even when she is dealing with the most abstract of propositions. Nor does she *stop* in order to know: she continues. (2007: 1, original italics)

Such an understanding explains rather well how people were able to know through their experiences of the garden, and what on the basis of those ways of knowing they were able to imagine. Local residents were driven to be interested in the garden project for various reasons. These included wishing to make it a place that they could walk through as a shortcut to town, fears about vandalism and its potential misuse as a dis-used and overgrown site. To a certain degree, these motivations were based on embodied knowledge, and the experience of 'being there'. For example, the first time I went to visit David and his wife Anne to learn about the garden project, we initially spent some time going through the plans for the garden and talking in their home before David and I ventured out into the garden in the rain with the video camera. At one point during this first tour, David asked me if I had been able to imagine what the garden was like before being in it, and I had to admit that I had not, until that point shared this tacit knowledge of, for instance, why one would really not want to walk through the wet grass of this shortcut in the rain (see also Pink 2008c).

Therefore, these explanations indicated that people wanted to feel differently about the field (i.e. not to fear vandals and such like, or imagine that a block of flats might be built on it) and they wanted the field to feel different when they walked in it. Thus the concern was with the material and affective transformation of the experience of the garden. Taking this as a starting point, the garden's transformation can be understood as a process of sensorial and embodied engagements (gardening, walking though the garden, stopping and talking in it, etc.), and other imaginative and practical activity (planning, applying for funding, etc.) designed to change the way that the garden might be experienced/known. All of these practices – gardening, planning, imagining, moving through the garden and socialising – can be seen as practices through which the garden both as a materiality and as a project was known and constituted. They are moreover sensorial and affective practices, involving making the garden feel different, feeling good in it and using it as a way of materialising one's feelings. Below I discuss two practices through which this was achieved, which are inevitably inseparable from the others: gardening and walking.

THE MULTISENSORY ENGAGEMENTS OF THE PRACTICE OF GARDENING

There is a small, yet interesting, ethnographic literature about gardens, gardening and their meanings in modern cultures including in Britain, France and Sweden (e.g. Chevalier 1995, Tilley 2006, Degnen 2009). Gardening has been understood as a multisensory, affective, embodied practice. For example, reflecting on research with gardens in Sweden and in Britain, Chris Tilley has pointed to the sensory and emotional aspects of gardening (Tilley 2006: 312) and argues that 'Our primordial relationship with the garden is through our sensing and sensed carnal bodies, a world of embodied perception in which we are not separate from the garden around us' (2006: 329). Here Tilley is actually discussing the relationship between the multisensoriality of the gardener's experience and the limited way in which this is articulated verbally. He suggests that 'It is the intimacy of bodily contact through all the senses, rarely put into words, or even thought about, that can be readily observed when you study the manner in which gardeners garden', in 'how they actually garden and care for the plants, *and the manner in which they walk about their gardens and remark about particular things in them*' (Tilley 2006: 328, my italics). In his emphasis on how gardeners know in movement, Tilley's analysis concurs with Harris's (2007) points (see above). Indeed this interpretation was borne out as I discussed and explored the garden and its gardening with David on video and during a photographic visit when he moved plants from a neighbour's garden into the community garden.

Resonating with Tilley's points, David's verbal articulations about the garden and his embodied navigation of the plants as he talked to me about them, led me to an appreciation of the way in which he was engaged with the plants through an embodied and practical knowing that could be better performed when moving through the garden with the plants, than spoken. Thus, by exploring the garden with him, I was able to learn about his *way of being with the plants*. This almost always involved touching the plants as a way of telling me about them, even when this was part of a video tour rather than actually gardening in my presence. The affective dimensions of interrelationships between people and plants is indeed implied in other existing anthropological work on gardening. Degnen suggests that 'connections between people and plants are not necessarily metaphorical but are instead reciprocal and social, embedded in a long history of significance' (2009: 165), and Tilley goes as far as to propose that 'The relationship between gardener and garden is … truly akin to that between lovers' (2006: 329).

Thus these sorts of embodied and affective relationships to plants also imply social relationships. Indeed during my research it was precisely descriptions of the social relations of planting – from persons to seeds to pots to garden – the funding and other achievements in developing the garden, and the persons and socialities these processes nurtured, that could be spoken about. This means that to a certain extent some tacit knowledge and practice is distributed – some gardeners are more experienced or 'better' at some things than others. It also means that gardening, in this case, is an inevitably social process that not only interweaves the trajectories of people and things but is also a more complex entanglement in a number of ways. Thus the garden project can be characterised as a process or event that has involved the coming together, the passing 'entanglements' of (for instance) gardeners, fundraisers, supporters, money, plants, tools, plans, and ways of knowing about this particular garden and gardening in general. It has involved the mobilisation of existing relations and the production of new socialities. It involves the material crafting of the garden and its placeness in terms of its rootedness in the earth. But while the garden as a materiality is visible as a locality, the community garden project is not a bounded entity; indeed its edges, although defined by the fences that separate it from private gardens, are open to plants, seats, paint, persons, services (i.e. water) that are moved between the borders, as well as to the weather (see Ingold 2008).

Therefore, thinking of gardening as a practice requires considering how it is not simply something that is done to and in gardens. Indeed the idea of boundaries and borders is problematised when we start to think about the relationships between people and gardens and between gardens and what is outside them. While we might map boundaries, to actually understand the meaning of the garden it is better to think in terms of how the practice of gardening creates trajectories, movements, constellations and entanglements. For example, elsewhere I have discussed how plants are donated, and moved from other mapped gardens into a community garden site (Pink 2008b): their trajectories are meaningful as they do not bring with them just leaves and roots, but affective qualities standing for the person whose garden they have come from, the socialities and embodied labour of their movement. Similarly, in Britain, Degnen has found that 'Gardens and plants are autobiographical, with individual plants having social genealogies in the life of the gardener as gardeners gift cuttings of plants to each other' (2009: 162). For example, when David showed me the daisies that had been planted in the flower bed, he was sure to mention that an elderly woman who lived nearby had donated them from her garden, and other plants reminded him of the persons who had planted them. The migrating plants contribute to this intensity, which is concentrated in the garden site (see also Pink 2008b). These practices of sharing and donating plants and seeds are not routine everyday (or daily) practices. Yet because the garden is now available as a destination for plants from other gardens, the moving of plants to it might become part of another gardening practice – for instance of moving plants that are no longer needed or wanted elsewhere. Gardeners also come and go. During each of my visits to the garden with David, he recounted to me how participants in the garden project had left or joined the committee, moved into the area, moved away, relinquished their roles or become newly involved.

Thus it becomes possible to conceptualise the garden as an experienced locality, as constantly emerging from this biography of the intersecting lives of the persons and plants that are not bounded by the fences that surround it.

As I have discussed above, things and persons are constantly travelling in and out of the garden's uneven rectangle. This does not simply involve the gifting of flowers and the donation of labour. It also includes, for example, the harvesting and consumption of a crop of mushrooms that unexpectedly grew in what had been understood to be sterilised fertiliser; and the replication of the design of its brick weave path in a resident's garden. As this makes it clear, the project of the garden as a place-event reaches its intensity *in* the rectangle, but is not bounded by it. Neither is the garden simply a recipient of 'things'. It is also a provider of inspiration, plants, feelings to take home, relationships to nurture, and through a formal assessment of the skills that it enabled participants to develop, even a provider of adult learning opportunities.

WALKING THROUGH THE GARDEN

Walking has also come to be understood as an everyday practice involved in the constitution or making of place, initially by de Certeau (1984) and more recently in the work of Gray (2003) and Lee and Ingold (2006). There has recently developed a focus on the ethnography of walking, its sociality and multisensoriality (e.g. Ingold and Lee Vergunst 2008, Pink 2009b). Above I noted how once the path was laid people could be observed taking it through the garden instead of being prevented from crossing it because of the wet grass (Pink 2007e). The planning of the path was one of the first activities of the committee. At our first meeting, David and Anne showed me a set of photos of the kind of brickweave path they had chosen and told me the committee members had even been on a trip to see samples. David later sent me a set of photos of the path being laid. Moreover, the path did not 'end in the garden', but, as noted above, there was a migration of its brickweave style.

Indeed the garden is *part of a route* to the town; people usually move in or through it, if they are walking along the path or if they are gardening in it. It is also somewhere people can temporarily sit in to rest. Things move in and out of its fenced surround, to and from it, meaning it might be conceptualised as a place that both extends from and extends into the town and into homes, by means of its affective and material dimensions as well as in the imagination. So, while as a researcher going to find out about what had been happening to the garden, I initially imagined myself as *going to* the garden, I was in fact missing the point. The garden would be more likely to be experienced locally as *being part of a pathway* or for those who garden as a place of intensities where they interact with plants, with the environment more broadly and with those whose pathways cross theirs. Indeed David told me he never lets anyone go across the field without stopping them and trying to involve them in donating labour or plants to the garden. His encounters with people going 'through' the garden have led to further investment 'in' the garden as these people have returned to donate plants, and more (see Pink 2008b). These initial path-crossings create further intensities as people, plants, embodied practices and their affects come into contact with each other. The garden can thus be seen as a domain of the criss-crossing of routes in the sense of the entanglements of 'lines' that Ingold (2007) writes about, for example not only of people walking through, but also of the intersections between the routes of someone slowly gardening and another meandering through with a dog or stopping to rest on one of its benches on the way home from shopping. These interactions are thus intersections between persons and between practices that are contingent on and constitutive of place. They contribute to the entanglement of routes that creates an intensity of place.

Understanding the garden as a series of routes, rather than as a bounded locality, also enables an understanding of how it has been transformed through practices of gardening and walking. Residents wanted the field to be a garden that could be traversed on foot. Once it was gardened and had become a route, it felt different; it was no longer a threatening or worrying piece of wasteland. Moreover, for some, it became a domain of personal investment that stretched the affective and material dimensions of self and home.

THE INVISIBLE INTENSITIES OF THE GARDEN

The approach developed above understands the experience of the garden in terms of the material, sensory and affective qualities of movements and entanglements of humans, plants, earth and more through which it is made. However, these experiential aspects of the garden are also constituted in relation to discourses, intentionalities, agencies and (not least economic) power. The garden's development has been contingent on diverse funding sources, the political will of the town council by whom the land is administered, and the practical facilitation of a charity.

If the community garden is theorised as a place, it can be understood as the intensified entanglement of humans, everyday practices, plants, earth, soil, fences, animals, seats, designs, borders, beds, flows of capital, political processes and ideologies, and more. Some such flows might be defined as 'local' and others as 'global'. Some are immediately visible to the researcher's eye or sensed by her or himself as they move through the garden. However, other flows that also determine how the uneven rectangle of the garden as a material locality is experienced are invisible yet likewise entangled in the processes through which the garden is constituted as a place.

THE COMMUNITY GARDEN AS AN ACTIVIST PROJECT

As I noted above, Aylsham is a member town of Cittaslow, an urban social movement. Town councils hold the membership of the movement and work towards maintaining and improving their scores against a set of criteria provided by Cittaslow, concerning a range of broadly environmental issues. I learnt about the garden project through my contact with the movement's leaders, and thus always understood it as being part of the town's Cittaslow identity. When I asked Jenny (vice-chair of ACT) if she thought Cittaslow has influenced the projects ACT had taken on, she told me: 'Yes we wouldn't be looking at a community garden if it wasn't for Cittaslow. I think it's fair to say that was the kind of light coming on, you know: well yes, if all that's happening and it makes that much difference, we should be joining the party and doing something with it. Although ACT has its own agenda in terms of supporting people, it's no different to that of Cittaslow really in that it's engaging the widest possible community in some form of mutual activity.' The community garden conforms to Cittaslow's principles and therefore the people involved in the practical task of making the garden were thus engaged in producing qualities associated with the movement. While most were neither expertly versed in its principles and ideologies nor active campaigners, importantly their goals coincided with Cittaslow's, thus supporting the town's claim to 'already' be a Cittaslow town, as opposed to Cittaslow being *done to* the town as a top-down town council driven initiative.

In the context of its contribution to and framing by the Cittaslow agenda, the garden project could be interpreted as part of what Parkins and Craig referred to as 'a site where agency can be exercised in the face of global culture' (2006: 83). To some extent this argument holds in that the garden represents a local, neighbourhood-driven appropriation of land, that one might imagine having otherwise been developed for financial gains. Yet it is important to also attend to the detail of how, within such processes, 'local' and 'global' flows become co-implicated. Indeed, thinking in terms of the entanglements (Ingold 2008) of place helps us to understand some of the complexities and apparent contradictions that contemporary forms of activism cannot avoid engagements with.

GLOBAL FINANCIAL FLOWS AND THE GARDEN

When we conceptualise space as plural (Massey 2005), this does not mean that spatial realities involve separate but parallel strands. Global flows that we might appear to be able to classify as being of different types – such as those of the flows of finance from business in contrast to those of the Cittaslow movement – are often better understood as being entangled with each other in complex ways involving interdependencies and ironies. British Cittaslow towns are a good example. In a Cittaslow town, many things that would seem to be opposed to Cittaslow principles inevitably form a part of the town, as well as being implicated in the ways that Cittaslow projects are mobilised. For example, most Cittaslow towns have big supermarkets owned by global chains. Moreover, it would be hard for even the Cittaslow leaders in such towns to live their lives without encountering these strands of the economy. Most readily admit to going to the supermarkets to buy domestic items not easily obtained from local independent traders. The garden is no exception.

On one of my visits to see David and to tour the garden, he first went through their funding successes with me. They had secured funding from diverse sources including a large bank as well as donations from local businesses and charitable groups and public sector organisations. In 2006 Anne and David wrote to me at Loughborough University with the news that the project had been awarded a donation from money raised as part of a recycling scheme from a big supermarket chain and that David and Jenny from ACT would be attending its presentation. These donations enabled the committee to purchase and install items such as benches, wooden surrounds for the flowerbeds and a proposed new section of pathway. The possibility of buying these items and their incorporation in the garden enables the emergence of new social–material–sensory–affective relations.

THE IRONIC ENTANGLEMENTS OF PLACE

I have stressed the experiential, multisensorial and affective dimensions of the garden as a place-event that is produced by and engaged with through living bodies. The various flows and movements that produced these are embedded in this experience, thus as we toured the garden David reminded me where the funding had come from for different parts of the garden, who had worked on it with him and who had donated the seeds and plants now growing in the garden. To use Ingold's (2008) term, it started to become clear how the physical garden could be experienced as a point in the biographical 'entanglement' of the flows through which its different resources of labour, plants, bricks, wood and other materialities had arrived. Indeed the affective dimension of the experienced garden is also contingent on these entangled flows. I opened this chapter by recounting how David had told me he felt 'proud' as he looked back over the garden site, two years since our first tour. The achievements of the garden are not just to do with the physical labour that the residents had put into the garden, but with the success of their funding applications and the council's approval of and support for their plans.

Some might regard funding from global businesses such as supermarket chains and banks being used to support a project that forms part of the Cittaslow identity of a town as an irony. However, I believe that it is better seen as an inevitability that is emblematic of a context where organisations standing for global businesses and urban social movements operate in a domain in which their trajectories are entangled. While Cittaslow activists are often critical when discussing the impacts of supermarket strategies on small independent retailers and producers (see Pink 2009b), they are not engaged in direct action against supermarkets. Indeed, in at least one Cittaslow town, a supermarket stocks local produce and, in another, a large supermarket chain store regularly announces the town's farmers' markets.

The community garden process thus becomes an example of how the global politics and flows, ideologies and materialities are involved in the production of what on the face of it is a local garden. On the one hand, we might assume that without the power of money and the persuasiveness of discourse and ideology, the garden may have remained a field. Yet, on the other hand, it is by understanding the motivations and satisfactions associated with the transition from field to garden through the question of the sensory embodied practices and experiences through which it became meaningful to local people that we can understand why it was made. In this chapter I have demonstrated some of the complexities through which both anti-globalisation and capitalist global flows are implicated in the everydayness of the phenomenological realities through which people might experience the local. This leads to the observation that neighbourhood-level sustainability initiatives might be understood at the intersection between the practice of everyday life, activism and global flows. The example discussed here suggests we may usefully build on the themes that dominate the existing literature about community gardens to analyse them as social and community-forming processes, and in terms of their local health benefits, and that to understand how these come about and how sustainability is achieved we might also attend analytically to examining the multiple flows and intersections of the performances of practices through which they are constituted.

CONCLUSION

Whereas in Chapters 4 and 5 I progressively focused on the constitution of the kitchen and then the sensory home, in this chapter I have shifted the focus to explore how an analysis of practice and place might be applied to the complexity of a neighbourhood project. In this chapter I have suggested how a phenomenology of place can enable us to comprehend how 'local' people experience, construct, understand and embed meaning in specific localities. Yet these experiences cannot be understood in isolation from global ideological and material flows. Understanding these processes as forms of 'entanglement' allows us to acknowledge how human perception, everyday practice, movement and global flows co-constitute place. An analytical focus on the intersections of practice and the innovations in its performance and the movement of persons, things, resources and funds, allows us to comprehend this complexity and produce an understanding of how a sustainable project has come into being and how it is maintained. As I have demonstrated, analytical attention to how human and non-human, local and global, and visible and invisible constituents are co-implicated in the processes through which place is constituted, invites us to consider how the experiential and the political intersect in processes of change.

7

(RE)MAKING TOWNS: SUSTAINABLE ACTIVIST PLACES, PRACTICES AND REPRESENTATIONS

'Because Slow, really, as you know, in cittàslow is not really about yokel slow is it, it's about quality and about caring' (Mo Reynolds, Aylsham (UK) Town Clerk)

'[slow living] involves the conscious negotiation of the different temporalities which make up our everyday lives, deriving from a commitment to occupy time more attentively' and 'mindfully' (Parkins 2004: 364)

Figure 7.1   Arrival scenes: traffic slowing/slow traffic

One of the first things I notice when driving into Aylsham, a small town in North Norfolk, England, with a population of about 6,000, are the road traffic speed signs. The closer one gets to the town centre by car the slower the speed limit, reducing further from the normal

30mph for built-up areas to a more unusual 20mph. Slow road traffic speeds, however, only express part of what 'slow' in the slow movement means. The term slow refers not to simply reducing the speed at which one travels or does things, but to the quality of life; as Mo, the town clerk, put it: 'Because Slow, really, as you know, in Cittaslow is not really about yokel slow is it, it's about quality and about caring' (Figure 7.1). In more academic terms, the cultural studies scholar Wendy Parkins has expressed a similar point in that '[slow living] involves the conscious negotiation of the different temporalities which make up our everyday lives, deriving from a commitment to occupy time more attentively' and 'mindfully' (Parkins 2004: 364) (see also Pink 2008c: 143–4 for a discussion of Figure 7.1 as a representation). Yet setting the speed limit at 20mph is within the powers of the Cittaslow-informed town council, and in doing so they are also representing the philosophy of the movement, in that slower traffic creates a safer, better environment. Moreover, the experience of driving into Aylsham, and one's arrival into the town centre, is shaped by the practice of driving slowly. The speed, which may be experientially unusual for drivers from elsewhere, becomes a component of the way of being in the town. It forms the way one initially moves through the town (the practice of driving in the town) and by going slowly drivers already participate in the making of the town as Cittaslow. The making of a particular quality of locality by regulating types of movement is not unusual in towns committed to a sustainability agenda. In 2006 I visited Orvieto in Italy, a founding member town of the Cittaslow movement. Here, as Knox and Mayer also describe, 'sustainable transport' is key to the town (2009: 48). Its historical centre is closed to cars, which are left parked below the plateau on which the town is located. Visitors can ride up in elevators or the funicular (see also Knox and Mayer 2009), making for a particular sensory experience of arrival.

INTRODUCTION

This chapter furthers the theoretical analysis of practice and place established in the preceding chapters through an exploration of how conscious, thought-out activism is engaged in urban environments. I focus on an examination of town-based activism and the flows of persons and things that are implicated in it. In doing so I offer a new perspective on an established theme: the sociologist Manuel Castells has urged scholars to develop an 'exploration of the environmental movement, and of an ecological view of social organisation, as urban areas become connecting points between the global issues posed by environmentalism and the local experience though which people at large assess their quality of life' (2002 [2000]: 402). In this chapter I follow Castell's focus on the urban, yet recognising that in fact most populations of under 500,000 'live in cities with fewer than 100,000 people' (Clark 2003: 27, see also Bell and Jayne 2007: 2), I depart from the emphasis in urban studies on world cities. Instead, following the (re)emergence of academic interest in the town (e.g. Bell and Jayne 2007, Knox and Mayer 2009) as a key context for analysing social and cultural change, my focus is on smaller urban settlements. Internationally Paul Knox and Heike Mayer tell us that 'Many towns are connected to others and are engaged in a global dialogue about sustainability and what it means to their future' (2009: 9). They outline how a number of networks concerned with issues of health and environmental stability have emerged in recent years. For example, 'by 2008 there were more than 1,200 European towns and cities designated as WHO [World Health Organization] Healthy Cities' and the principles of the Eco-City movement have influenced the design of new towns, for example in China, the United Arab Emirates and Japan (2009: 40–1). In the UK, with the emergence of eco towns, transition towns and Cittaslow, there is an increasing presence of town-based sustainability agendas and networks such as UK Action for Market Towns Network, which research participants spoke of (and is discussed by Knox and Mayer 2009: 42) and which also connects towns. This context calls for an academic focus on smaller urban settlements as sites of activism and change, and thus a reworking of the question of how local activism is also *part of* being global.

In this chapter I draw on ethnographic research as well as post-ethnographic online follow-up research, to consider how towns are (re) constituted according to activist and sustainability agendas, again building the analysis through a consideration of practice and place. I take Massey's notion of the 'event of place' as the starting point for my analysis, thus treating the constitution of the town through its Cittaslow qualities as an ongoing 'constellation of processes' (Massey 2005: 141) in which places are 'articulations within the wider power-geometries of space' (2005: 131). However building on the focus in earlier chapters on the experience of place, human perception and movement which draws more closely on Ingold's (2007, 2008) understanding of place I combine this with an examination of how a particular urban sensory aesthetic is implicated in the making of Cittaslow towns. I also account for practices as an entry point into understanding urban sustainability processes in two ways. First, I consider the activist practices of local councillors and Cittaslow committee members who lead town policy making, such as sitting on committees, public speaking or cooking at public events. These are both ways of embodied being and thought-out applications of the movement's principles and are played out at an intersection between discourses, the materiality and sensoriality of the town, socialities and representations. Second, I discuss the Slow movement's agenda to make interventions that enable and encourage sustainable everyday life practices among local residents. Thus I reflect on how activists create social, material and technological interventions in towns and, by implication, change (possibilities for) residents' imagined and actual everyday practices. These include projects ranging from making available local produce, plastic-bag-free campaigns, road traffic speed slowing, use of public 'spaces', and representations including photographic exhibitions, 'community' digital media archives and web pages.

However, because Cittaslow has a wider agenda as a transnational social movement, the implications of activists' practices go beyond the activists' own towns. Massey has suggested that not only world cities but 'all places … have lines that run out from them: trade routes, investments, political and cultural influences, the outward connections of the internal multiplicity itself; power relations of all sorts that run around the globe …' (2007: 7). Massey's proposal, moreover, makes an ethical argument, which stresses not only the impact of the local beyond its immediate environs, but also the 'responsibility' this carries (2007: 15). She asks: 'If actions and policies adopted within one place negatively affect people elsewhere, what responsibility is involved, and what accountability? (2007: 15). In the case of environmental activism that spans the local and global, the question shifts slightly, since by engaging with environmental movements in local contexts activists tend to already take a responsibility for 'place beyond place'. For instance, Cittaslow activists expand their experience of the local through their contacts with the Cittaslow 'network', since the 'constellation of processes' (Massey 2005: 141) that makes a town Cittaslow includes not only local processes but also those associated with its international centre, and a form of relationality with other member towns.

THINKING ABOUT CITTASLOW ACTIVISM AND EVERYDAY LIFE

The Cittaslow movement was established in Italy in 1999 by a group of Italian mayors, along with Carlo Petrini, the leader of the eco-gastronomic movement Slow Food, seeking to apply the principles of Slow Food to urban living. The movement is growing globally and by 2010 had 133 member towns in 20 countries (see http://www.cittaslow.org for up-to-date information). Cittaslow ascribes to a broadly environmentalist and local produce-based agenda and a programme for local urban governance aimed at improving local quality of life, maintaining local uniqueness and supporting sustainable urban economies. It was created as a response to what its founders perceive as the contemporary 'fast' and globally homogenising world. Cittaslow member towns must have populations of under 50,000 (although other entities and organisations can join the 'network' as Cittaslow Supporters) and through a focus on 'small realities in a more and more global connected world' (http://cittaslow.blogspot.com/2008/10/philosophy.html), the movement promotes a local urban distinctiveness. Both Slow Food and Cittaslow seek to make interventions in everyday life practices – by educating people to appreciate the local, to live in ways that are environmentally sustainable, promote local economies, source local produce, and more, and to celebrate these markers of locality. For instance, Slow Food seeks to intervene in everyday life practice, by inviting shifts in how ordinary consumers shop, cook, eat and appreciate local produce. It promotes gastronomic culture, taste education and agricultural bio-diversity, protects at-risk foods, has its own university, and publishes books and a journal. Slow Food urges individuals to integrate its principles into their everyday practices and expects its members (private individuals who meet in groups called *convivia*) to promote these values through projects (e.g. in schools, with local producers). As Parkins and Craig point out, Slow Food 'not only seeks to intervene in public discourse and policy but also to foster a different approach to everyday life amongst its supporters' (2006: 32). This is most clearly seen in the movement's 'taste education' agenda. As stated on the Slow Food website:

> Taste Education helps people to make daily choices about food with awareness and responsibility, turning the consumer into a co-producer, becoming an individual engine of true change, choosing Good, Clean and Fair food.

And

> Slow Food learning communities stimulate a real and much needed 'cultural revolution' through food by changing the mentality of ordinary consumers and their relationship with food. (http://www.slowfood.com/education/welcome_eng.lasso)

As part of its template for sustainable urban governance, Cittaslow incorporates a commitment to Slow Food's concerns, to promoting changes in individuals' and groups' everyday practices and providing channels for transnational connections and knowledge exchange. To achieve this and its other sustainability goals, Cittaslow disseminates among its global members a model for local governance. In developing these localised interventions in small towns across the world, the movement seeks to resist some forms of globalisation. In existing analyses of its development in Italy and Germany, it is regarded as providing a successful model for sustainable local development (e.g. Knox 2005, Mayer and Knox 2006, Parkins and Craig 2006, Knox and Mayer 2009). In the UK, Cittaslow is being recognised in the public imagination alongside other movements as a route to sustainable living. For instance, in 2009, I was invited to speak about Cittaslow at a public event (Grand Designs Live at the National Exhibition Centre, Birmingham, England) alongside speakers on the transition movement and eco towns.

The accreditation process for Cittaslow member towns requires them to score over 50% in a self-assessment process, against almost 60 specified criteria concerning its environmental and infrastructure policies, the quality of urban fabric, encouraging local produce, hospitality and community, and creation of Cittaslow awareness, as well as undergoing an inspection. Significantly, town councils rather than individuals become members of Cittaslow. Thus the movement and its agenda become part of local government, which enables the flows of its discourses, examples of good practice, and more to move across public institutions and have broader influence (see Pink 2009b). Within the movement's national networks, national and regional lead towns link the member towns and the international network and base in Italy, as well as being involved in the accreditation of new members. There are some variations as the movement is adapted to different national systems, as demonstrated by existing studies of Cittaslow in Germany (Mayer and Knox 2006), Italy (Parkins and Craig 2006, Miele 2008, Knox and Mayer 2009), and moreover, individual towns work towards the common goals of the movement in ways specific to their own situations. For instance, Mara Miele (2008) has shown variations in how slowness is articulated and engaged in, in relation to its alternatives between the two towns she analysed in Italy. Likewise, British Cittaslow towns develop in locally specific ways (see Pink 2009b). The UK Cittaslow network was established in 2004 in Ludlow, where it held its base until 2009, when it moved to Perth in Scotland. Ludlow and three member towns – Aylsham (2004) and Diss (2006) in Norfolk, England and Mold in Wales (2006) – figured in the research carried out between 2005 and 2007 and discussed below. In 2010 there were nine UK Cittaslow member towns, tending to be historic market towns, usually with populations of between 6,000 and 11,000. At first glance Cittaslow towns might appear affluent and middle-class, with their delis, cafés and restaurants. Yet further ethnographic attention to the practices and places of activism in Cittaslow towns offers a different interpretation. They are towns where some small businesses thrive but others struggle (and some close down), where, like anywhere, there can be problems of unemployment, where ordinary people set up cooperatives to cut food costs and air miles, and where low-energy light bulbs save costs. Being slow does not necessarily implicate people into buying more costly products.

Cittaslow's approach, like Slow Food's, involves the *indirect* activism of demonstrating by example rather than direct confrontation. From the 'flexible action repertoires' of contemporary urban social movements (Mayer 2006: 203), they select negotiation over marching and 'pragmatic' over 'militant' strategies. Comparing Slow Food to the direct action of the anti-globalisation movement, Carlo Petrini, the leader of Slow Food, stressed that 'Our choice is to focus our energies on saving things that are headed for extinction instead of hounding the new ones we dislike' (2001: 26). The statements of Cittaslow leaders around the UK were consistent with this approach, stressing how the point of Cittaslow was to demonstrate the alternative and better ways of doing things to those presented by global corporate capitalism, and thus convince local people to live their everyday lives according to the Cittaslow philosophy (see Pink 2009b). In existing publications I have discussed how Cittaslow achieves this through an analysis of town-based events, projects and activities, including amateur photography practices (Pink 2011a), carnivals (Pink 2007c), committees (Pink 2008b), skill-building and food projects (Pink 2008a) and the issues big supermarket chains raise for small towns (Pink 2009b). In Chapter 6 I showed how a sustainable community garden project can contribute to the constitution of a town as Cittaslow. In this chapter my focus is broader. Focusing mainly on one UK town, Aylsham, complemented with examples from other towns internationally, I examine selected examples of how the Cittaslow qualities of towns are created. I discuss how these facilitate alternative multisensory and social experiences, and how they offer possibilities for the performance of sustainable everyday life practices. Collectively these interrelated processes maintain the Cittaslow identities of towns, and enable them to participate as part of the movement's international network, thus involving them in global processes.

A FOUNDING TRADITION: THE BIG SLOW BREAKFAST

Before the 20mph signs shown in Figure 7.1 came into being, in October 2004 Aylsham's first Big Slow Breakfast was served. This was the town's founding moment as a Cittaslow member and is repeated annually although in ways that have changed over the years. The event usually provided a full cooked and continental breakfast for 150 people at two sittings, although (as Mo told me by email) in 2010 this changed slightly with 'one rolling sitting throughout the morning'. The breakfast is based almost entirely on local produce (with a few necessary exceptions) and cooked by the town's Slow Food group. Like the meals I participated in in Diss and Mold, following Slow Food principles, the event creates a context where people can share and appreciate the tastes of locally produced foods in a convivial environment, which is not excessively costly (tickets were £3). The events are attended by a selection of the town's (predominantly white British) population, including families and older people and crossing socio-economic classes. In 2005 and 2006 I attended two Big Slow Breakfasts, held in different buildings in the town. The 2004 founding Breakfast was never distant. It was recounted to me by research participants in our interviews and the photograph of the late Massimo Borri (Director of Cittaslow's International Network) eating a traditional English breakfast while seated in the town's main square, presented on the town's web presence, was a constant reminder of the event's significance (http://www.cittaslow.org.uk/towninfo.php?Tid=2 &Pid1=16&Pid2=16&PLv=1). Below I describe my experience of moving through the 2005 breakfast as a researcher to show how the breakfast can be understood both as an experimental environment and as a place that is constituted through diverse components. Put simply it involves an intensity of persons, foods, ideologies, discourses, furniture, skilled practices, cameras and images. All in movement, and co-implicated to greater or lesser extents as they proceed in relation to each other.

I switched on the video camera as I walked, with my family, to the hall where the breakfast was in progress. As I went I recorded the route into the building, the locality and the signage for the event. As I moved through different social intensities, the camera was switched on and off, the absences standing not for moments that were irrelevant but for those where I had still not asked the people around me if they were happy for me to video-record them as I entered the hall. As the anthropological filmmaker and theorist David MacDougall has argued, when we make images 'They are, in a sense, mirrors of our bodies, replicating the whole of the body's activity, with its physical movements, its shifting attention, and its conflicting impulses towards order and disorder'. MacDougall thus directs our attention to not simply the question of what images are 'of' in the sense of their content but the idea that 'they are also images of the body behind the camera and its relations with the world' (2005: 3). This brings to the fore in different ways, through presence and absences, the sociality and sensoriality of place that are implicated in the experience and actions of the camera(person) in movement. I switched the camera back on as I encountered Vanessa making finishing touches to the buffet table, where the cold breakfast items were laid out. These included locally made croissants and other pastries, jams, cereals and more. As Sue, who was at the time in the kitchen, had told me in our first interview, it was only the orange juice that, understandably, was imported. The table was now being prepared for the second sitting, which I would join as a breakfaster later. Vanessa (who is very active in local organisations and activities) updated me on the social composition and good atmosphere of the first sitting as I video-recorded. I started to have a feeling of being at and being carried forward with an ongoing event.

As I walked on with the camera into the kitchen, the sense of activity, sociality and sensoriality became more intense. Members of the Slow Food convivium were preparing the cooked English breakfasts to be served to the next cohort of breakfasters. Sue, the first person I had made contact with when I started researching, Cittaslow, was standing at a big sink wearing much-needed rubber gloves as she washed up big baking trays with the hot steam rising from them, obscuring her from the camera as she worked. Nothing was static in the kitchen as the equipment was washed, the tomatoes baked, and later on the fresh local eggs and bacon fried on the hob and transferred to plates as the first guests started to arrive at the hatch to order and collect their meals. The kitchen was in progress, it was moving forward. People completed tasks and moved on to new ones, foods were prepared and transferred to trays, to the oven and to plates. Washing up arrived and was processed. Steam, cooking smells, conversation and laughter created a constantly changing sensory blend that as I moved around with the camera in the kitchen, I was also part of. After a time, Liz, who is the leader of the Aylsham Cittaslow Committee and chairperson of the town council, told me she had time for us to have the short interview we had been trying to schedule for some time. We walked over to the empty seats towards the end of the hall, and, as I recorded her, Liz narrated the developments in and her views on the town's Cittaslow identity and activity. Our interview ended as the hall started to fill with people and sound and we both became subject to other demands. I returned to the kitchen where food was now being served, following the activity there as it became both more intense and seemingly more routine as a set of practices for serving were established and repeated in similar ways. I left the kitchen, on my way recording the activity around the cold buffet table, and returned to our seats and settled down to share the local tastes and produce with my fellow breakfasters. The camera was off and my partner and I chatted to our co-breakfasters, engaging in the sociality of the 'shared table' that is part of the Slow Food philosophy. As we progressed through the meal, there was a pause for Liz's second performance of her speech, which focused on the town's Cittaslow events and achievements during the year, including a reference back to the breakfast Massimo Borri had attended, local and international achievements, and plans for the following year. Liz's speech formed one layer of representation at the breakfast. In addition to this were exhibits of local produce and a digital photography slide show projection. Thus representations, discourses, senses and socialities all form part of the experience of place and the constitution of the town's identity through this event.

The practices of cooking, eating, tasting, socialising and speaking all involve some human actions and movement. While photographs might initially be thought of as static texts, if they are re-conceptualised as being produced and viewed as part of a world in movement, their role as representations can be understood as part of the event of place. The very idea of a slide show implies some kind of movement. When viewing the slide show at the Big Slow Breakfast, I knew that I was viewing a sequence of images that are somehow intentionally related to each other and to the context. Slide shows invite us to a journey, moving from one image to another spaced in a rhythm that one quickly comes to anticipate. The point about slide shows is that they involve a visual narrative with which the viewer moves, going forward into the potential offered by each image and its relationship with the next. Even if the slide show is in a loop, just as it is not possible to go back to a place one has been in before (see Massey 2005: 124), when the beginning point of one's personal loop recurs the slide show cannot ever be viewed *again*. Rather, it is always and inevitably viewed *anew*, with the experience of what has gone before.

When we consider how the images in the slide show cohere with the slow ideology, the activity in the kitchen, the local tastes of the breakfast, the sociality of the slow-food style of 'shared table' and the talk given by Liz, we can start to think of them as not so much representing a slow ideology, but as being part of a process through which the viewer moves forward and knows in an environment (as developed in the works of Ingold (e.g. 2000) and Harris (2007) discussed in Chapter 2). The images in the slide show are not themselves ideological – they do not inherently carry a 'slow food' discourse. They were part of a wider ecology of place where vision did not necessarily dominate, in that slowness was experienced through a multisensory environment which also involved experiences of food, conversation and more. Understanding them as such enables us to define them as participants in a process through which a particular ideology was sensorially, socially, verbally and visually infused through its relationality with other constituents of place. Thus the images were implicated in the making of meaning by moving together and being intertwined with these other elements of place.

This celebration of Aylsham's founding moment as a Cittaslow town therefore is annually reinforced and has created a historical process, which is self-referential. It is an (invented) tradition, which creates a

public experiential representation of the meaning of the Cittaslow identity of the town. It therefore makes and reaffirms the town as Cittaslow,
through an annually repeated set of interconnected practices performed
by different players – the cooks, the organisers, the breakfasters. As a
food-related event, the breakfast is of further significance because it also
promotes links to other food activities in the town. The most relevant of
this is perhaps the regular farmers' markets that promote connections
between local producers and consumers, along with the presence of the
three local butchers' shops from whom the sausages and bacon were
sourced. The presence of local food traders is essential to the town's
emphasis on locality and on supporting local businesses and local
producers; it is also part of the town's indirect activism against global
business entities. In this context the breakfast can be seen as an intensity
of place where these philosophies, socialities, economies and experiences
are brought together in a way that exemplifies Cittaslow and at the same
time *promotes* the everyday practices it seeks to engender. Above I have
focused on the experiential and reflexive as well as processual elements
of the constitution of a Cittaslow event, which can only be recounted
on the basis of the researcher's first-hand experience. Yet it is equally
possible to imagine how similar configurations of Cittaslow activities
and discourses can become phenomenological realities in other national
contexts. For instance, Knox and Mayer describe how in the German
Cittaslow town, Hersbruck, there is an 'initiative aimed at linking the
cultural landscape with community economic development' by promoting
'the use of local produce in traditional region-specific dishes and
restaurants'. In this case producers and consumers are connected as
'the farmers supply the restaurants with their seasonal products and the
restaurants offer special menus that also indentify the producers by name
and location for the benefit of the consumer' (Knox and Mayer 2009: 139).
Here, as for Aylsham, flows of produce, social relations and tastes of the
local become intertwined with the ideologies of Cittaslow.

HISTORIES, MEMORIES AND BIOGRAPHIES: THE PERSONAL AND THE COLLECTIVE IN CITTASLOW CARNIVAL

Aylsham carnival was re-established, after a five-year lapse, by the town's
Cittaslow committee as part of its annual calendar. In 2005 I participated
in the carnival with my video camera, talking with, and when appropriate, video recording the words and activities of some people I had already
met and interviewed and others who became further involved in

the research over the next two years. The carnival consists of a series of carefully coordinated activities and events that fill the main square, a historic side street and the town hall, which faces onto the main square. Like the Big Slow Breakfast, it can be understood as a multisensory event that offers local people a festive experience of the town framed by Cittaslow principles. For example, only locally sourced foods are on sale, and the live music and performances are by local artists (see Pink 2007c). As such carnival does not permanently occupy or claim the town but rather offers participants a route through the town framed by an alternative discourse and set of experiences to those associated with the global supermarket chains that also have a presence in Cittaslow towns. It is created in a context of co-existence of these different agencies, and can be seen as both an experiential event and as a series of (convincing) representations of the Cittaslow way. Such events offer possibilities for the co-existence or intersections of different types of practices of (audio)visual production and representation. In this section I focus on how, on the one hand, the representational and the experiential and, on the other, the personal and the collective become interwoven in the production of a biographically reinforced sense of Cittaslow identity.

During the 2005 carnival, present-day photography was accompanied by a theme that brought images, memories and local identity to the fore through an exhibition and projections of digital/digitalised photographs from the town's archives. These images on one level narrated local history to local people (and to visitors like myself). Whether or not it was intended, the exhibitions and slide shows can be interpreted as having the effect of endorsing the historical embeddedness of carnival in the town (similar historical endorsements were achieved in different ways in later carnivals, for instance by re-instituting an historical carnival game). The 2005 carnival exhibition was multifaceted. In the main hall, tables were laid out with copies of numerous photographs taken during past carnivals from 1933 to 1987 (Figure 7.2) with the perhaps predictable content of carnival queens, groups of men wearing carnival disguises, and more. As I 'hung around' at the exhibition with my video camera, a Cittaslow committee member recounted to me how she had gone up into her loft to seek photos to contribute to the exhibition, she said it had been 'worth it', hoped they would be archived and offered to find more for the archivist who participated in our conversation. These photographs were not necessarily all amateur images. Some came from the organiser's own collection, others he had been given by friends and made copies of, and some represented professional and official documentation of the carnival. They are nevertheless interesting as a whole due to the ambiguous mix in the culturally established ways the images encouraged people to engage with them. On the one hand, this entailed

Figure 7.2 Images of past carnivals were laid out on tables during carnival. This meant that local people could scan for relatives and friends, and remember past events together, to produce personal narratives and collective memories at a number of levels. Photograph © Sarah Pink 2005, with credit to Aylsham Town Council Archive to which the photographs featured in this figure belong

the type of memory practices and personalisation associated with a family album or personal photography collection. On the other hand, the images formed part of an effort to create a public and collective set of memories of carnivals past. In this sense, the personal experiences invested in the photographs and the biographies of the people (living and deceased) represented could be seen as contextualised in terms of the history of carnival. With my video camera, I was taken by two participants to see photographs – for example, an elderly man whose wife had been a carnival queen in the 1950s, took me to her portrait. In these participants' comments, the sentiment of personal good feelings about aspects in past carnivals was bound up through the photographs in the experience of the present carnival.

The exhibition was therefore collective in several senses: local people had contributed to its composition; it was viewed not by individuals in isolation, but as part of the carnival crowds as they entered the hall; and it invited people to set their own memories in a wider visual context. The event was also participatory in further ways. In another room of the hall, a local history project (the COMA project) that supported the town's Cittaslow identity was presented. As part of this project, local people bring in their photographs and they are digitally scanned into an archive that was being shown as a slide show. O a table nearby were copies of photographs from the archive, copied on sheets of paper with spaces added for local people to identify and write in the names of the people represented. This involved local people in the collective task of building this history – as Mo, the town clerk, told me it was a process through which they might be able to track a person right through 'from a little girl to a grown woman'.

Photographs can be very relevant in terms of how they integrate personal narratives into the constitution of a history for a public event. If we understand carnival through a theory of place then we can see how the photographs form part of a visual-sensory-material environment in which people become engaged. The viewing practices were also contextual, involving a particular form of participation in a public context alongside others engaged in similar activity. When we therefore start to think of the phenomenology of carnival as a multisensory event, we can situate these visual-sensory practices of viewing, touching and moving around in relation to images as an experiential context where personal narratives are invoked, materialised and connected to a public context, being converted into local history and thus having potential to stand for a type of collective identity through the images. The effect is thus to invite people to (re)imagine the past in the present and to connect personal, family and historical narratives with the contemporary Cittaslow identity of the town – something which itself is symbolised by its Cittaslow carnival. Thus (remembered/imagined) embodied and affective experiences associated with the moments in which images were taken are thus represented in the present. Indeed because Cittaslow towns are intended to be 'better' for people to live in, it is important to be able to demonstrate the personal implications of Cittaslow projects for individuals.

URBAN MATERIALS AND MATERIALITIES

The elimination of plastic bags from towns and cities internationally is becoming an increasingly recurring theme. It is also a project that is coherent with the principles of Cittaslow and through this example I now consider how towns might become imbued with the movement's principles through such material shifts. The plastic-bag-free-Aylsham campaign was initiated on 3 May 2008 (Figure 7.3) and Aylsham became the first plastic-bag-free town in Norfolk (although others had already been established in the UK). This was after my fieldwork in Aylsham but I was able to follow events online and through my continued contact with those involved with Cittaslow.

Figure 7.3 The Aylsham plastic bag free poster is reproduced on the website shown on the poster with the caption 'When you are shopping in Aylsham, look for this poster. Traders who are supporting the scheme will be displaying this poster in their windows.' © Norfolk County Council, with many thanks to Cittàslow Aylsham, Aylsham Town Council, Broadland District Council and Norfolk County Council for permission to reproduce this image

The campaign in the town was accompanied by a web presence (http://aylshamplasticbagfree.blogspot.com/) as well as the poster above. The process to be followed to introduce the plastic–bag–free initiative was described on the blog as follows:

> Norfolk County Council are providing one free shopping bag to each household in Aylsham. These will be available to be picked up from the market place of Aylsham on Saturday 3rd and Saturday 17th May. Times and other information will be announced nearer the time.

Broadland District Council are supplying recycle bins around Aylsham town centre for visitors and businesses to recycle their plastic bags. The aim of the whole scheme is to remove plastic bags from the system, because they are damaging to the environment. We want to encourage everyone to stop using them, especially for lining their bins at home, which means they definitely go to landfill.

Therefore, one element of this involved the County Council providing local residents with free (non-plastic) shopping bags, thus encouraging the practice of using the new bags. Another entailed the District Council collecting those existing plastic bags and attempting to eliminate them from the town and discouraging habitual practices such as their use for lining bins as well as for shopping.

Different individuals and households will inevitably engage with this process in diverse ways, yet it is possible to interpret this intervention in relation to how towns are constituted as places. The anti-plastic-bag policy invites new practices, ways of experiencing, urban flows and materialities as one element of the material culture of everyday life is actively displaced and another introduced. It changes the material configuration of the town, in the sorts of materials that are circulating in it, and simultaneously introduces an ideologically imbued set of practices that can be interpreted as referents to Cittaslow discourse, whether or not they are self-consciously thought out as such by the users of the new bags. The policy also has additional effects in that it reduces, however slightly, the market for plastic bags in the town, thus curtailing in its small way elements of the global flow of these materials. In Aylsham, therefore, the materiality of Cittaslow is made explicit through this public plastic-bag-free campaign. It is a materiality of flows, constantly shifting as different types of bags are taken on different routes through the town. Like the encouragement of local produce, which involves flows of foods and persons through the town, it is not pitched as a direct form of activism against globalisation, but rather as an alternative way.

The shifting materialities of Cittaslow towns are also represented in the construction, restoration and use of buildings in the towns. For example, for three years from 2006 in Diss, a Cittaslow shop and office was set up in a unit in one of the town's historical courtyards, while funded through a European grant. The shop served as a central point for granting Cittaslow funds, selling local products and the administration of Cittaslow projects in the town. In Aylsham new public toilets were built near the main square, working with an architectural design that it was felt was appropriate to the Cittaslow status of the town. In Diss, a Cittaslow project involved the production and use of traditional local clay lump bricks, which are used in the repair and maintenance of traditional historical buildings in the town. Here again, the practice of producing and working with the bricks, the material flow of them into the town and their presence in its building structures, creates an interwoveness of Cittaslow principles with the very materiality of the town, part of the entanglement of discourse, materiality and practice in the configuration of place.

ACTIVISM FOR THE GLOBAL LOCAL

As the examples above and the analysis in Chapter 6 show, a range of quite different projects, events and activities are produced in the making and maintaining of Cittaslow towns. These are not evenly replicated across UK Cittaslow towns, and likewise, as others have shown, in Cittaslow towns in Italy (Miele 2008), Germany (Mayer and Knox 2006) and more widely (Knox and Mayer 2009), the Cittaslow principles are engaged in context-specific ways. Yet, common ways of creating Cittaslowness in these towns can be seen to operate by involving flows of people, discourses and things that make and move with representations. Becoming Cittaslow is both a political and phenomenological process and therefore both levels of analysis are needed to understand its implications. It shifts the way everyday life can be experienced in the town, but it also has economic implications and a policy agenda. By locating member towns with the wider movement they become 'activist' towns. It is in this sense that we can think about the activist processes in the town as having a broader responsibility – through an activism that is not just concerned with 'our town' and the protection of their own 'local' but the idea of the wider protection of a global local.

Malpass, Cloke, Barnett and Clarke have argued, through an analysis of the Fair Trade City campaign in Bristol (UK), that Massey's understanding of 'place beyond place' offers a useful way to understand local activism that has wider (global) implications. The Fair Trade movement is different from Cittaslow in that while Cittaslow's emphasis is on sourcing produce locally, Fair Trade is concerned with supporting local producers in poorer countries by trading with them in ethical ways. 'The FTC [Fair Trade City] campaign deploys spatial imaginaries of local and global in distinct ways. Not only is the emphasis on the overriding objective to improve the position of poor and marginalised producers in the developing world (FTF 2002) but there is also a clear intention to re-envisage and if necessary "support" the local' (Malpass et al. 2007: 640). Yet Cittaslow towns can be interpreted as equally unbounded – the difference is in the nature of the flows. On the one hand, Cittaslow towns seek to spread the Cittaslow framework to the local elsewhere. The

Cittaslow model is understood as a successful urban sustainable development model (at least as applied to modern Western societies) and the towns that figured in my research made and received visits to and from Cittaslow groups from Asian and European countries. For example, I was invited to speak at a conference in Ludlow, at which examples of Cittaslow projects were disseminated to a delegation of visitors from local authorities and academic institutions in Catalonia. On the other hand, one would expect the Cittaslow focus on responsible consumption, local produce and sustainable materials to have implications in relation to the demand for transportation, fuel and mass-produced materials.

URBAN ACTIVIST PRACTICES AND PLACES

An analysis of slow urban activism raises the question of how we might understand the activist practices of those who are simultaneously working towards protecting what they perceive as traditional while embracing what they regard as positive forces of change. Cittaslow activism is without doubt an explicit thought-out process that depends on the embedding of an adherence to its guiding principles in everyday life routine practices. One appeal of the movement is that it is seen as a means of protecting towns that are already perceived to be undergoing processes of change, but not in such a way that is against change of all kinds. The ways that 'traditional' practices are (re)created in the everyday possibilities for local residents do not reproduce 'traditional' normative behaviours and moralities. Rather, they reinterpret 'traditional' ways of being in relation to new (and perceived as desirable) components of everyday life, including new media and technologies, and in relation to a global environmental sustainability narrative.

The discourse of Cittaslow is one of interweaving – the combination of the best of the old with the best of the new. Activists often told me that their towns had 'always been Cittaslow', thus claiming an historic embeddedness of the principles that the movement refers to while also engaging the 'new' as part of their policies. The practices of activists are explicitly informed by Cittaslow principles as they develop local government and connect it to the Cittaslow framework. The example of the Big Slow Breakfast brings together in one event the sociality, sensoriality and emphasis on locality that are so central to the movement's work. Here a series of practices – of local produce, cooking together, eating together, public speaking, digital representation and digital visual production – came together to interweave the 'old' and the 'new'. By moving *through* the event with the camera, I was able to chart its progress as I went. Indeed, each of the events I have discussed in this chapter involves a series of interweavings that forms part of the wider 'constellation of processes' (Massey 2005: 141) through which the Cittaslow qualities of towns are constituted. This analysis might equally be applied to Aylsham, the main example discussed above, the other UK towns in which I did ethnographic research and the examples from other national contexts. For instance, Knox and Mayer describe how a series of four projects in Hersbruck, Germany, involving local foods, educational activities and uses of local wood, each connects 'the environment with the local economy' (2009: 139) in different ways. In the experience of my own ethnographic research as shown above, such sets of projects can create an ecology of processes that are interrelated, and in terms of representations are inter-represented. Such an analysis allows us to explain the relationships between embodied knowing, discourse and representation that have been demonstrated in the examples discussed above. It connects experiential realities with policy processes. It also demonstrates how participation in locality-based practices that form part of a wider place, have implications for other related places and the localities with which they are entangled. They are part of a place that extends beyond a fixed locality.

CONCLUSION

In Chapters 4 to 6, I have shown how by taking the sensory aesthetic of a room, the home, or garden as a starting point for understanding place as experienced and practised, we can achieve a route to knowledge that situates the practice of everyday life in relation to the wider ecologies it is part of. In this chapter, I have built on these arguments to examine how the town, its physical locality, the flows of things, persons and discourses that intersect and become interwoven in relation to its administrative boundaries and the practices that are co-implicated with these, become entangled as constituents in the making of towns.

Therefore, if we take as our starting point an understanding of towns as place-events and multisensory environments that can be experienced in relation to a series of alternatives, then this provides a route to analysing how sustainability agendas are constructed and experienced. As a place a Cittaslow town can be understood as an intersection of the movement's principles, the spatial and physical environment of the town, flows of people, traffic and goods, and much more. The practices of Cittaslow activists – which emerge as, for instance, policies, events, physical structures and sensory environments – thus arrange or influence the qualities and nature of these components to the different degrees that they are able to. These create everyday and/or festive environments that are imbued with the movement's principles. The possibilities for the way people might experience and perform everyday practices as part of these environments are thus framed by qualities associated with Cittaslow, and as I showed in Chapter 4, this can also be translated into the way individuals might shop and cook. Yet as Chapters 4 and 5 also made clear, individuals navigate place and innovate as they perform practices in ways that are contingent on multiple elements. Therefore this does not mean that the application of a sustainability agenda in a town as such will simply change, from above, the everyday practices of local people. My point is rather that, by approaching the ways that sustainability agendas are produced in towns through an analysis of practice and place, we are able to discern how possibilities for sustainable consumption are generated and the ways these are related to the experience of moving through and being part of a town.

8

THE DIGITAL PLACES OF EVERYDAY LIFE: THINKING ABOUT ACTIVISM AND THE INTERNET

Once I had clicked on the 'Like' icon on the Cittaslow International Facebook page, I began to receive status posts from the movement (publically available at http://www.Facebook.com/cittaslow). Most were in Italian, although some were in English. They alerted me to media reports about Italian Cittaslow towns, less frequently to events and activities in Cittaslow member towns elsewhere, and the up-and-coming international 'Cittaslow Sunday' to be held on 26 September 2010 in member towns across the globe. The day after I joined, I received the news post that the Facebook page now had over 1,500 fans. I started to feel a new closeness to the organisation as it became an everyday part of my online life on Facebook and I felt a shifting sense of its global reach beyond what I had experienced when visiting its Italian headquarters and the UK Cittaslow towns.

Activist Facebook posts would rarely be the only news that the followers of any group receive. They would therefore be resituated uniquely on each individual home page to which they are posted. For example, the Cittaslow Sunday post that appeared on my own home page was immediately followed by a post from the UK based nef (new economics foundation). The nef describes itself as 'an independent think-and-do tank that inspires and demonstrates real economic well-being' (http://www.neweconomics.org/about). In this particular post its director, Andrew Sims, proclaimed that 'We've gone into the ecological red'. This news indeed sounded serious. I followed the link to nef's website where Sims went on to write that:

> At the weekend, Saturday 21 August to be precise, the world as a whole went into 'ecological debt'.

That means in effect that from now until the end of the year, humanity will be consuming more natural resources and producing more waste than the forests, fields and fisheries of the world can replace and absorb. By doing so, the life–support systems that we all depend on are worn ever thinner. Farms become less productive, fish populations crash and climate regulating forests decline. All become less resilient in the face of extreme weather events. (http://www.neweconomics.org/blog/2010/08/23/weve-gone-into-the-ecological-red)

Thinking back to the time I had spent in Cittaslow towns in the UK, these two narratives became interwoven in my own story. I started to contemplate how (as stated on the Cittaslow website) the 'mayors, the citizens and the partners of the 130 associated Cittaslow [towns] scattered in different countries' were working towards, in a small 'slow' way, addressing an enormous issue – through their aim for what the movement referred to as '"positive contamination" regarding the little Cittaslow, the big metropolis and the entire society, with positive effects on the overall ecologic imprint of the world human activities' (http://www.cittaslow.org/index.php?method=attivita&action=zoom&id=96). Or, putting it another way, I began to consider how interventions at the level of everyday life practice are implicated in the process of creating a more sustainable environment in this context. Because this is one of the issues this book is concerned with, it is not surprising that it framed my reading of the two status posts and the other online texts and discourses they were linked to. Yet this was just my own personal encounter and interweaving of two publically available pieces of Facebook post as they landed on my home page. I appreciated them alone, unaware if the same two pieces of news would be similarly juxtaposed on the pages of other Facebook users (whose affective experience of them would indeed have been different). My experience was moreover part of my own digital everyday normality where diverse narratives become juxtaposed, intertwined and participate in mutual meaning making as I move through the everyday. In this chapter I examine how we might extend the understanding of place engaged in previous chapters to encompass the role the Internet and digital technologies play in everyday life.

INTRODUCTION

Digital media are increasingly central to everyday life experiences, activities and environments, although unevenly and in different ways among different individuals, groups and regions of the world. Indeed the ethnographer of everyday life is more likely than not to encounter digital media as implicated in the practices and places that she or he focuses on. As we saw in Chapters 4 and 5, media form part of everyday life practices in the home and, as domestic engagements with digital media increase, this is a growing research area. Likewise media were embedded in the local Cittaslow projects discussed in Chapters 6 and 7, where digital photography and non-web-based computing were part of the community garden project, carnival and breakfasting events. Cittaslow places, like any other place, are not simply localities. Rather, they span the Web and are thus implicated in a further public domain and set of relationalities both through the Cittaslow International web presence and because Cittaslow towns each have their own websites (although the content and detail varies among towns).

The increasing prevalence of Internet technologies in everyday life raises the question of how we might interpret this reality analytically in a way that is coherent with the approach developed in this book. In the preceding chapters I have applied an approach that focuses on practices and places to understand ethnographic realities, researched through face-to-face contact with people in their homes, a neighbourhood and towns. In this chapter I explore how this approach might be applied to understand how the Internet might participate in the constitution of place. In doing so I focus on the example of the Cittaslow web presence to explore how mediated and global digital activism can be interwoven with everyday Internet platforms. There is a thriving literature on doing ethnography on the Internet, in the form of virtual ethnography (Hine 2000), netnography (Kozinets 2010), online visual ethnography (Ardévol 2012) and the sensoriality of doing ethnography online (Pink 2012), which would be relevant to further investigation in this field. However, here my intention is not ethnographic, but rather I seek to set the stage for creating connections between the ethnographic approach to everyday life outlined in the previous chapters and a way of understanding how the Internet can be implicated in the constitution of place.

My concern in this chapter is therefore to examine how we might theorise the digital presence of an organisation in a way that is compatible with the understanding of the contexts of everyday life that I have promoted in the previous chapters. Recognising that the ways a web presence is experienced will be diverse and multiple, my focus in this chapter is on developing an online analysis rather than an analysis of the specificity and multisensoriality of online/offline relations and contexts as they are lived (although I consider the latter elsewhere – see Pink 2012). Rather, I suggest a way of approaching the online elements of place that one would experience multisensorially. As I emphasised in the opening example of this chapter, our experiences of online representations and of their relationality can be highly contingent. If there is an ethnographic or experiential approach to this chapter, it is that of my own implicit auto–ethnography of my experiences of the Internet. Indeed methodologically it is relevant to acknowledge this authorial subjectivity. This is especially so given the often unexplained dimension of 'our' or a general experience of new media that sometimes enters theoretical discussions. Indeed I invite readers to likewise reflect on their own experiences in engaging with the web locations and platforms discussed in this chapter, as part of the process of 'reading'.

In developing this approach I consider how a focus on the relationality that characterises theories of place, rather than the connectivity that is often the focus of Internet studies, invites an alternative and complementary perspective on the more conventional use of network theory for understanding digital activism. Taking existing Cittaslow web contexts as an example, I explore how we might theorise the web platforms that can potentially become part of everyday life. Such an approach is not *an account of* everyday life, and that is not my intention here. Rather, I seek to set the scene by proposing a way to theorise the technologies that enter into the experience of everyday life through the example of my encounters with the online components of the Cittaslow web presence. The analysis is, however, ethnographically informed, in that it is based on understandings of the Cittaslow movement, its work and localities that are rooted in my face-to-face ethnographic engagements with persons and towns in the UK and Italy.

My approach also involves engaging as a researcher with texts and representations, which as I have argued in Chapters 2 and 3, are both part of and produced through everyday life and activism. While the content of these representations is of interest, it is not my primary focus. Rather, I consider how web-based representations are implicated in and emergent from relations, how they are at once parts of media ecologies and constituents of place, and how they become the basis for our imaginations. Therefore I take the online platforms and texts that are the material for analysis here to be the outcomes of activist practices, in that they are digital representations *made* by activists and informed by their principles. Yet they are not the products of activism alone, but are in fact contingent on the possibilities of software, agendas of corporations and forms of online regulation. Therefore my analysis also explores the nature of these representations as constantly evolving technologies. Moreover, it is not simply the process of technological change that makes our everyday experience of web-based media contingent. Rather, it is the human participation in web platforms that also means that as representations web pages are not static, but their content is often constantly and visibly changing.

In the next section I set out how understandings of place, as discussed in Chapter 2, might be engaged to understand the Internet, before then demonstrating these principles through an analysis of Cittaslow International's online presence.

UNDERSTANDING DIGITAL NETWORKS THROUGH PRACTICE AND PLACE

'Network' has become a dominant analytical concept in Internet studies (see also Postill 2008). Activists refer to their movement's 'network' as their organisations develop national and global connections and relationships, and the use of web-based media certainly has implications for how their perceptions, actual practices and representations of networking develop, as well as for the subsequent effectiveness of the network that is produced or supported through digital media practices. For academics 'network' is a theoretical concept developed and applied in a number of guises to various social and material phenomena, including digital media (e.g. Castells 1996, 2004) and visual media and culture (e.g. Mirzoeff 2002). It is moreover a contested concept, and before considering how it might be engaged in relation to a theory of place, I discuss how these disagreements are played out.

For Castells, whose understanding of networks is highly influential, 'A network society is a society whose social structure is made of networks powered by microelectronics-based information and communication technologies', thus 'A network is a set of interconnected nodes'; it 'has no centre, just nodes'. He gives primacy to networks in that 'Nodes only exist and function as components of networks' and they are deleted when they 'become redundant' (2004: 3). Castells moreover argues that this is a historical departure in that 'what is actually new both technologically and socially, is a society built around microelectronics-based information technologies' (2004: 7). Outlining the implications of his theory of a network society, he emphasises the importance of making 'the networking capacity of institutions, organisations and social actors, both locally and globally' central to the analysis (2004: 42), stressing how 'connectivity and access to networks become essential' (2004: 42). Castells' notion of the network society is a powerful conceptual tool that is engaged by theorists as well as academic-activists (e.g. Juris 2008), who bridge the divide between those who want to produce social interventions as well as analyse them. Yet often attention to ethnographic detail in less mainstream places rocks the certainty of social theory and thus some anthropologists have cautioned against a network approach. For instance, Miller suggests that network approaches 'envisage that the modern (or to use that most banal of academic terms, the post-modern) world exists principally in a more direct relationship between individuals on the one

127

hand and a global network on the other' (Miller 2011: 190). His own research, about Facebook in Trinidad, Miller argues, does not support this argument since such extremes do not exist. Likewise rooting his approach in ethnographic research about Internet use in local government and everyday activism in suburban Malaysia, Postill has suggested that what he calls 'a field of residential affairs', better describes the situation he encountered than do the dominant concepts of community and network (2008: 422), to show how relationships are actually played out. From a different anthropological perspective, Ingold (2008) also questions the understanding of the relatedness of things in terms of networks. He argues, as I outlined in Chapter 2, that we should think of the environment of which we are a part as a 'meshwork', in order to understand 'organisms being constituted within a relational field'. The distinction from a network is significant in that by a relational field Ingold means 'a field not of connectable points but of interwoven lines, not a network but a meshwork' (Ingold 2008: 1805). Thus things are not related because they are 'networked', as Ingold argues:

the relation is not *between* one thing and another – between the organism 'here' and the environment 'there'. It is, rather, a trail *along* which life is lived. (Ingold 2011: 69, original italics)

Neither beginning here and ending there nor vice versa, the trail winds through, or *amidst*, without beginning or end. (Ingold 2008: 1805, original italics)

This emphasis on relatedness rather than on the connectedness of discrete entities also resonates with Massey's notion of place as 'open to the externally relational' (2005: 183). Massey, however, applies the ideas to understanding the relationship between the local and the global. She argues that:

An understanding of the world in terms of relationality, and world in which the local and global really are 'mutually constituted', renders untenable these kinds of separation. The 'lived reality of our everyday lives' is utterly dispersed, unlocalised, in its sources and in its repercussions. The degree of dispersion, the stretching, may vary dramatically between social groups, but the point is that the geography will not be simply territorial. (2005: 184)

These understandings raise new questions about how digital and social media are part of environments and experiential fields that are part of everyday life and activist practice. They invite us to consider the relationality between people, pages, software or towns beyond the idea of their 'being connected' and through an understanding of them as they '*really* are "mutually constituted"' (Massey 2005: 184, my italics).

Yet while these anthropological and geographical critiques suggest alternative routes to analysing the relatedness of digital elements of the work of activist groups or movements, Castells' notion of network society (e.g. 2004) remains relevant. This is not least because notions of network already inform how some movements and organisations are represented. It moreover invites us to research how activists might structure, perceive and enact connectedness, and the actual implications of this for particular movements. A network approach thus provides us with a certain way of understanding how and why connections or relations *do* become essential for movements (see Castells 2004: 42). Yet to understand the sensoriality and experiential elements, the sociality and relationality involved in the ways web-based media are implicated in the practices and places of everyday life, other theoretical approaches need to be engaged. For example, this can be seen in the work of the anthropologist/activist Jeff Juris, in his study of anti-globalisation activists in Barcelona. Juris treats network as a central theoretical frame, yet he discusses how he developed a study not of a network itself but, he writes, of 'the concrete practices through which such networks are constituted'. Juris suggests that 'contemporary activist networks are fluid processes, not rigid structures' (2008: 5). The notion of network is also central to the way Cittaslow's organisation is represented and conceptualised online, as I discuss below, and there is certainly a dimension in which the type of connectedness it represents is important. The question this raises, I believe, is not so much one of whether a network approach is right or wrong, but of how what activists themselves call networks are lived, represented and experienced, through the multisensory, experiential, embodied and everyday practice, and as part of place. From this perspective, Chapter 7 showed how being part of a network becomes part of the phenomenology of an urban ecology of place. In this chapter I analyse how the web presence of an organisation that calls itself a network can be understood through the relationality of place.

PRACTICE, PLACE AND MEDIATED ENVIRONMENTS

In recent years, practice and spatial 'turns' have had increasing impact across disciplines and thus media scholars have also begun to engage further with concepts of practice and place. For example, Nick Couldry and Anna McCarthy (2004) propose the concept of 'MediaSpace'. This they describe as 'a dialectical concept, encompassing both the kinds of spaces created by media, and the effects that existing spatial arrangements have on media forms as they materialise in everyday life' (2004: 2). As a way of thinking about what constitutes MediaSpace, Couldry and McCarthy stress its multidimensionality. On the one hand, there is its materiality – it is 'composed of objects (receivers, screens, cables, servers, transmitters), embedded in particular geographical power structures … and reflective of particular economic sectors in capitalism'. On the other hand, they emphasise its virtuality – the 'anti-concrete sense of spatiality'. Thus: 'MediaSpace, then, at once defines the artefactual existence of media forms within social space, the links that media objects forge *between* spaces, and the (no less real) cultural visions of a physical space transcended by technology and emergent virtual pathways of communication' (2004: 3). These ideas invite us to consider how media likewise might be understood as part of the places of everyday life, as well as their implications for the way we experience spatiality in everyday contexts. Here, following the work of Ingold (2007, 2008) and Massey (2005) outlined in Chapter 2, I understand the places in which media participate as likewise open, unbounded, constituted as an event and constantly shifting. In Chapter 7, I have already considered how media contribute to the processes of making place in towns, and there the role of media in the making of places that incorporate elements from other localities and historical periods or moments was evident. Indeed understanding media through a theory of place, reminds us further of the nature of place as non-locality based. It enables us to understand media practices as *part of* places that incorporate localities yet extend beyond them, and indeed to see media practices as part of the process through which places bring together materially, geographically and temporally diverse phenomena. Recently a number of scholars (see Lapenta 2011, 2012, Pink 2011a, Uricchio 2011) have begun to explore the implications of digital visual and locative technologies for social and environmental relations. As this work shows, Web 2.0 and related developments enable new configurations and experiences of place.

Alongside this focus on the spatiality of (new) media, has been a growing interest among media scholars in theories of practice. On the one hand, the concept of practice has also been brought to the fore for the study of media through Couldry's focus on 'media practices' (Couldry 2004). On the other hand, there has been a growing focus on understanding media ethnographies through practice theory in the work of media anthropologists. Birgit Bräuchler and John Postill's edited volume *Theorising Media and Practice* (2010) includes Couldry's perspective in a collection that shows rather well how practice theory (in its diverse forms) might be engaged for the analysis of media across a range of contexts. Following the argument in Chapter 2, I suggest bringing these two moves towards spatial and practice theories in media studies together to situate media practices in relation to the contingencies of place.

By rethinking digital media through a theory of place, we can bring together the diverse processes in which media are implicated, the different media technologies and media practices involved and other constituents of place. Therefore, we can see these processes as being in/part of movement, and thus understand the interrelatedness of technologies, ways of accessing them, software, sensations, other practices, discourses, moralities and more with them. Much of what people (as individuals and as part of organisations) do online is increasingly multi-platform, and engages different platforms simultaneously as, for example, in the case of academic work where blogs, twitter, Facebook and academia.edu may be synchronised. This in itself signifies the need to think in terms of forms of interrelatedness, of practices, of online platforms and of the offline environment (and its affective, material and sensory dimensions) that any user is in at any time. As the example with which I opened this chapter showed, the qualities of the place of which I was a part depended on a series of processes that became interrelated, including the actual content of feeds to Facebook originating in different sources online, software and web platforms, energy flows, and my own ongoing interest in and practices of writing on specific issues. Yet it is not only the online context where we find this multiplicity, but also the technologies through which it interfaces with our everyday lives. I can connect to the Internet in multiple ways as I browse Facebook on the iPad as I sit on the sofa, use my laptop for more keyboard-related activities and then reconnect to the public Wi-Fi system to click on a link through my iPhone when I arrive at the municipal library. It is not only the continuities between the global and the local that come to the fore when we start to think about how activism and digital media interface. Rather, contemporary social media platforms and the technologies through which we access them make digital activism interweave with our everyday media practices and the environments in which we participate.

As I have stressed above, however, my focus in this chapter is less ambitious, in that my analysis focuses on understanding part of this configuration. In the following section I interrogate the online presence of the Cittaslow movement. My aim is to demonstrate how a theory of place might be applied to this digital context. Thus understanding it as always standing for a set of online constituents of a place that is open to the offline, and indeed that will be continually re-constituted as the online and offline are interwoven.

DIGITAL CITTASLOW: ANALYSING THE ONLINE CONSTITUENTS OF PLACE

The contemporary Cittaslow International site is part of a Web 2.0 context, a development from a former Web 1.0 website, and a blog (which at the time of writing remained online at http://cittaslow.blogspot. com/, accessed 10 November 2010, although its final entry was in 2009). In its current online presence, Cittaslow engages a series of different web platforms that cannot be understood as separate from each other, or from the face-to-face realities of the experience of Cittaslow in its offices, conferences and town-based activities discussed in Chapter 7. During the discussion below, I cite the web locations and recommend that readers visit these while engaging with the ideas presented. In what follows, I first discuss how the Cittaslow network is represented on its website, through text, hyperlinks and Google Earth, before focusing on two further elements – Facebook and YouTube.

The Cittaslow International website at http://www.cittaslow.net/ is presented in Italian and English, although these versions are not identical. It is an online domain that provides the main portal for first-time visitors. In this sense it can be usefully understood as a representation or as a series of interwoven strands of representation that are the outcomes of activist practices. As I argued in Chapter 7, representations are part of everyday life. They are produced and consumed as part of the everyday and their trajectories become intertwined with those of other things and persons as we move. It contains written details of the movement's philosophy, charter, its leaders, scientific committee, information about how to join and contact details, news and images. In this sense it is a reference resource, but also a campaigning tool. Yet the site is frequently updated and is therefore not static. The pages with more slowly changing content thus always exist *in relation to* those that are visibly constantly changing with, for instance, news items or details of new member towns.

As I pointed out above, the notion of network is not simply part of a theoretical agenda but part of the way social movements are understood and represented by activists. The notion of network is indeed part of the way Cittaslow is represented as an international organisation, its member towns become part of a network, and its online representation lends itself to this idea. In the words that alternate on the screen of the home page of its website in a series of different languages, Cittaslow is an 'International network of cities where the living is easy' (http://www. cittaslow.net/). Down the left-hand column, the international network is represented in the form of a list of links to pages concerning each of the national networks. Once links are followed outside the Cittaslow site, national and town specific sites are locally designed and in this sense vary in a way that corresponds to Cittaslow's appreciation of local uniqueness. They all, however, use the official Cittaslow logo and in some cases have English translations. To track the network online one may access it through Cittaslow international pages which link to national network pages, individual town pages through the links to national pages of the Cittaslow site, and to the email addresses of key Cittaslow personnel in the member towns and national networks. We can understand this bringing together of towns through a notion of network as creating a type of mediated relationality between towns.

Yet the current Cittaslow International site is much more than simply a representation of the network and a resource bank. It has some characteristics of a blog, others of the more fixed information pages that were part of its former Web 1.0 site, and is interwoven with a series of applications through links to its Facebook page, twitter feed and YouTube channel, as well as an e-newsletter that users can sign up for. These uses of social media are in some senses new but can be understood as coherent with Cittaslow's existing practices. As Andrea Mearns of the Cittaslow International Committee pointed out to me by email in 2011:

> Cittaslow has long recognised the importance of maintaining and creating public places for social contact and interaction. But only relatively recently have we actively used social networks to share ideas and information and to have a place beyond the constraints of miles, time and financial pressures.

The content of the Cittaslow International website includes formal information covering areas including the movement's history, principles (discussed in Chapter 7), how to join, its leaders and contact details. Yet its content is not wholly owner-driven, as contributors can fill in an online form to submit a Cittaslow event to the online calendar, and information is shared through its news section. The way that users can take navigational control over their own experience of the site is exemplified by its links to Google maps. Google maps can itself be seen as an everyday technology that has multiple uses, including that of organisations with an online presence which seek to visually geo-locate their presence digitally. Digital mapping is receiving increasing attention from media scholars who are interested in its dual identity as both a tool owned by a powerful corporation and as a participatory mapping medium (see Farman 2010). This apparent contradiction which is also at the core of debates about other contemporary web applications and platforms is particularly pertinent to the theme of everyday life and activism. In these existing critiques and debates, digital mapping is seen as a departure from the colonial history of cartography, both in terms of the ways its photographic qualities represent 'reality' and its participatory and social potentials (see Lapenta 2011 and Farman 2010 for theoretical discussions of these issues); thus entering everyday life as a medium and representation that has different qualities and experiential possibilities to that of conventional cartographies.

Cittaslow International uses Google maps to locate the existing Cittaslow towns, allowing users to locate and view towns using Google's satellite, map or earth functions. Although given that these are small rural towns, they do not necessarily have the photographic detail of Google maps or the Google Streetview coverage one expects for big cities in modern Western countries. The Google map image(s) engaged by Cittaslow international provide a map of the movement, from above, starting literally, if one clicks on the Google Earth option, with a global view. This perspective invites us to think of globally dispersed yet connected localities. Yet the use of digital mapping technologies that visually map from above and enable us to *move over* and *zoom into* localities is also multiperspectival. It does not create a commitment to just *one* location as being at the centre of the world. Rather, the user becomes centred and experientially browses *over*, in and out with the satellite images. Our use of Google maps is set within the frame determined by Google and the possibilities of its software. Yet it enables the world to be mapped according to its Cittaslow towns, all pinned onto a digital globe that may be rotated and approximated at the user's will. As such it invites us to 'see' and in some ways experience a representation of the globe in a particular way informed by a slow perspective. Yet these engagements are with representations that users encounter as they move across maps/through the Internet. As I argued in Chapter 3, representations form part of everyday life, and following Ingold (2010a) our encounters with them are with things that are 'like things in the world' (2010a: 16). When we engage with a digital Cittaslow map, we are experiencing what Lapenta emphasises is 'a synthesised image … a combination of contiguous photographs' (2011: 17) populated with pins that stand in the digital representations of the physical localities of Cittaslow towns.

The Cittaslow International website therefore can be seen as an intensity of hyperlinked representations and applications created through different media. Moreover, as such, it is not a bounded unit. Rather, it is open – unbounded – in that it extends *out* to map the movement and its network in a number of ways using digital mapping and through hyperlinks to the national and town-specific websites. Simultaneously it invites the representatives of the member towns to send *in* postings about events and activities. It also gathers and presents news and links to reports about Cittaslow elsewhere in its 'news' section, which as I discuss below are related to its Facebook feed. Yet the online dimension of the Cittaslow movement is nevertheless inseparable from the persons, materialities and representations that compose it. In this sense, it might be conceptualised as an intensity of human and technological processes that are interwoven with each other. If we think of them as the global-local, we can see that they can be simultaneously local and disparate from each other, and brought together as part of an intensity of things that together *are* a global movement. Understanding the website as such contributes further to a theorisation of it as part of a process of place. Although, as I have stressed already, the analysis does not account for how different users will engage with it, it invites us to consider place on two levels. First, to understand these technologies and representations as potential constituents of mediated elements of place and second, to contemplate how they engage users in the making of places that put the human subject at the centre.

Yet Cittaslow's online presence is implicated further in everyday life through the ways that it crosses platforms. As I discussed in the opening section to this chapter, Cittaslow's website is linked to the social networking platform, Facebook. The relationality between the movement, its news and Facebook is particularly relevant for understanding how activist news can become interwoven with everyday life media practices and mediated places. Therefore I first outline some key aspects of the relationship between this everyday social networking platform and activism. As for Google maps, discussed above, the relationship between social networking sites and activism is ambiguous in a number of ways. As Miller has put it, Facebook is often labelled as 'corporate' (2011: 196). Yet 'it does not follow, however, that because Facebook is a company, whatever anyone does with the web site it produces is somehow intrinsically "capitalist", "neo-liberal" or indeed "corporate"' (2011: 197). For example, as John Postill has noted (see http://johnpostill.wordpress. com/2011/04/29/presentation-notes-free-culture-activism-and-social-media-in-barcelona/) among free culture activists in Barcelona during his fieldwork in 2011, the use of Facebook, twitter and blogging platforms was often seen as a pragmatic solution, if somewhat ambiguous in relation to the movement's agenda.

Therefore as Miller has put it, 'the fact that activists clearly use Facebook, is not evidence that Facebook turns more people into activists' (Miller 2011: 189) and dana boyd has gone as far as to suggest that 'Activists have fantasized about ordinary citizens using SNSes for political action and speaking truth to power. Yet these daydreams are shattered through even a cursory look at actual practices' (2008: 112). Nevertheless activist and campaigning movements are using Facebook pages and when they do so their supporters (and researchers interested in them) rally to 'like' them, and subsequently usually receive posts about the activities of the organisation on their personal Facebook pages, which, as I have suggested above, interweaves these narratives with others of everyday life. On one level, this reflects a context where, as boyd (2008) suggests, people interact online with people (or in this case organisations) they already know, or have some connection with. For the purposes of the objectives of this chapter, this raises the question of how the uses of Facebook by such movements might make activism and everyday online life happen in one and the same place. In the opening section of this chapter I discussed my own experiences of the presence of Cittaslow posts in my Facebook newsfeed. Indeed these status posts become part of the everyday flow of Facebook, in that they are ongoing and bring 'news' from the movement to me, rather than being focused on one specific event. Thus, mediated activist and other narratives as we engage with social media in everyday life become interwoven.

However Facebook is not homogeneous in the way it is used and it is important therefore also to caution against seeing it as playing just one role in activism. As Miller argues, 'from an anthropological perspective it could be said that there is no longer any such thing as Facebook. There are only the particular genres of use that have developed for different peoples and regions' (2001: 188). Miller examines the local uses of Facebook in Trinidad – a field site that contests the idea that there is a normative Western (North American) Facebook practice. In the case of Trinidad Miller comments that 'there has been much enthusiasm for the more constant potential for activism facilitated by Facebook, and the example that came up several times in these portraits was the protest movement against the proposed aluminium smelter in Trinidad' (2011: 188). He comments that in this case, 'Facebook certainly was used to publicise such activism internationally and to coordinate activist events locally' (2011: 188). As a campaigning tool, therefore, Facebook is used in ways that are contingent on different types of campaigns and movements. Yet we might however speculate about its *character* in terms of understanding how it becomes part of everyday life, and as such a route through which campaigns reach everyday life contexts. Thus, theorising Facebook as a constantly shifting and distributedly unique representation, it is possible to start thinking of it on two levels. First, it can be seen as a representation though which users can imagine the realities that are referred to. Yet a Facebook page is neither static nor made up from one single source. On the one hand, it is framed by the agenda of the corporation and (the changing possibilities of) its software; on the other, it is filled with a dynamic and moving series of contributions from 'friends' and updates of the user's choosing, not to mention the content contributed by the user her/himself. It thus becomes, in ways remarkably parallel to Massey's (2005) theory of place, a set of stories or narratives that are often previously unrelated, are interwoven in a narrative set out on the screen of a computer or mobile device and that become lived and inter-preted by the user of that 'home page' as part of everyday life. It is within this 'meshwork' (to use Ingold's (2008) term) where narratives and rep-resentations intersect and become relational that Cittaslow status posts arrive on my personal page. As such we might understand Facebook as an everyday medium through which activism becomes entangled in our multisensory everyday worlds. And, moreover, through the comments function it invites us to further entangle ourselves.

A further dimension of Cittaslow's online presence is its YouTube chan-nel (publically available at http://www.youtube.com/cittaslownews). The videos uploaded to the channel include a range of media production and dissemination genres and practices from national mass media broadcasts, local promotional town-based videos, and handheld camera video inter-views with Cittaslow representatives at events, as well as what is seen as 'community heritage'. Examples of these are: video recordings of public speeches given at Cittaslow and Slow Food events and conferences; impromptu short interviews with Cittaslow leaders at international Cittaslow conferences; promotional and documentary videos portraying different Cittaslow towns in different countries (in some cases in English for an international audience); national television programmes that feature Cittaslow leaders, Cittaslow or other persons or themes related to Cittaslow and Cittaslow events and festivals; as well as other genres of short videos. As I argued in Chapter 3, video offers alternative routes to explor-ing, representing and empathising with human experience and material and sensory environments, as well as ways of associating these with verbal discourse. It thus invites viewers to a range of contingent and imaginative understandings. Therefore, on the one hand, we might analyse these videos through the idea of what Laura Marks has called 'haptic cinema' (2000), focusing on their capacity to invoke in the viewer imaginative and sensory experiences. As such, as a whole (which is constantly changing as new videos are uploaded), the video archive can be seen as a route to understanding/imagining the multisensoriality of diverse (but not system-atically covered) Cittaslow events, towns and experiences. On the other hand, following MacDougall's (2005) notion of 'corporeal cinema', we might moreover consider each video to stand for the sensory embodied experiences associated with the multiple positions from which these videos were shot. Yet significantly, and going beyond the parameters of both Marks's and MacDougall's approaches, these YouTube videos should be understood both in terms of their qualities as video, and as part of multimedia complexes and components of web archive. As part of multimedia sites they are also accompanied by the possibility of written comments and by records of the number of viewings they have had. Within the archive they are sortable and exist in relation to each other.

We might also begin to understand the international nature of Cittaslow through its YouTube channel. While many Cittaslow events are based in Italy and much of its coverage is in Italian, the interviews from events include a good range of countries and languages from Europe and beyond. On the YouTube channel, Cittaslow activists and towns are represented publically. For example, the short interviews with Cittaslow town leaders involved public figures making statements about Cittaslow, while news programmes are other contexts of public representation, as are conference talks and other similar events. Documentary and publicity-type videos likewise create representations of Cittaslow events and towns to a wider public. Therefore, to understand the Cittaslow YouTube channel, one needs to consider a range of potentials. These include the choices, nature and experiential possibilities invited by the videos as multisensory texts, the capacity of the user through her or his own practices of organising, sequencing, viewing and selecting videos to design her or his own experience of the videos as an archive. Moreover, viewers have the chance to participate through the possibility of contributing comments. The site is additionally an archive of representations, meaning that it offers the further analytical opportunity of asking how the movement's discourses are represented in the videos. The YouTube channel therefore provides a further way of thinking about how audio-visual representations and the ways that they refer to material localities and the persons featured in them become part of the way the work of an urban social movement is both performed and mediated online. The role of a video or set of videos in the making of a place is always contingent on the practices and other constituents of the context of viewing. Yet these videos are digital traces of, and *part of,* the Cittaslow identities of towns or the conferences and events at which they were filmed, rather than simply being representations of them.

The Cittaslow case is an example of a relatively new set of uses of digital media in activism, which have emerged between 2009 and 2010 as a shift between what has been called Web 1.0 and Web 2.0. It shows how multiple media, platforms and applications are brought together to create an online presence where these different elements are at once interwoven and yet remain open to the outside, as such they are potential constituents of place.

DIGITAL PRACTICES AND PLACES

It would be difficult to study contemporary everyday life, activism or sustainability agendas without understanding media as part of the places and practices with which they are involved. Moreover, attention to Internet and digital practices reinforces the point made in earlier chapters that it would be a mistake to depend on a notion of locality to understand how everyday life and activism are experienced. Rather, it is crucial to recognise that local places involve strands that originate from elsewhere and that are moreover multiply present elsewhere while being 'here' as well. In Chapters 6 and 7, I showed how discourses and flows originating from outside the immediate localities in which ethnographic fieldwork is experienced can nevertheless be understood as being part of and constitutive of experiential environments. Attention to the Internet and the way it forms part of activist places reinforces this point. The places of which the Internet is a part involve a complex interweaving of web platforms, representations, discourses, constantly changing content, online socialities, and material and sensory experiences of perhaps multiple localities. Indeed, when seeking to understand the digital dimensions of place, it is not simply the relationship between online and offline contexts that is relevant but also the cross-platform nature of digital practices and places. When it comes to discussing the places of online global – local activism, a focus on Facebook, twitter, websites, blogs and YouTube as separate platforms becomes redundant. When campaigning, movements may use these different platforms *in relation to each other*, or as already related. In this sense the focus must also incorporate how aggregators and inter-platform connections are part of the unbounded online – offline places of the everyday lives of an increasing number of ordinary people in the twenty-first century. Such mediated processes and contexts are inevitable elements of every-day life, and are as such inextricable from the practices and places where sustainability might be both lived and experienced and campaigned for.

CONCLUSION

The Internet, its representations and the different ways that people move through and engage with it, are integral to the processes through which it may become implicated in the making of interven-tions that will lead to a sustainable future. In this chapter I have examined how understandings of place as developed by Massey (2005) and Ingold (2007, 2008) might enable us to examine how the Internet and Web 2.0 contexts might meet everyday life and activism. In doing so I have suggested that Internet research, developed to acknowledge online – offline relationalities through a theory of place, might be framed in ways that are analytically coherent with similar approaches to interpreting kitchens, laundry, neighbourhoods and towns. Yet as I have demonstrated, such an approach also needs to be sensitive to the technological and representational qualities of online elements.

The implications of bringing together an approach to the Internet with the analysis of other domains of everyday life are both theoretical and methodological. An approach that understands media and its offline relationalities through theories of practice and place can bring us to an understanding of how human, technological, political, representational and other processes become interwoven. A methodology that understands the experiential, mobile and changing nature of such configurations offers a route to knowledge that comprehends how media are part of the flow of everyday life. Ethnographers of everyday life and activism increasingly traverse these online–offline worlds as they move through and make 'ethnographic places' (Pink 2009). A theoretical and methodological approach that focuses on practices and places, and interprets the Internet and representations in relation to these, invites us to begin to think analytically about how people might engage with them as routes through which to make meanings and imagine multisensory realities.

9

CONCLUSIONS:
SUSTAINABLE PLACES,
ACTIVIST PRACTICES AND
EVERYDAY LIFE

In this book I have engaged the concepts of practice and place as routes to understanding how everyday life can be situated within social, material, digital, sensory and environmental relations. My argument has been based on a commitment to understanding both practices and places as being open, defined in terms of their potentialities and characterised by movement. Whereas in some existing literatures practices and places have been theorised as having essential qualities and as such are used to describe and determine particular types of empirically observable activities and localities, here I have departed from such a way of thinking. Such understandings have often seen practices as sites of or vehicles for normativity or resistance and places have been determined through their social, material or symbolic dimensions. Here, conversely, I have argued that both place and practice should be treated as abstract concepts that might be engaged to understand a range of human activities and environments in such a way that does not predetermine our analysis of what types of outcomes or experiences should be associated with them.

Clearly however, no project is without its own agenda and in this book I have engaged these concepts specifically as a route through which to understand how experiential elements of both the activities and environments of everyday life might be implicated in activist processes and sustainability agendas. In doing so I have examined the practices and places of everyday life and activism through themes of multisensoriality, movement and representation. These three themes, I suggest, offer ways to trace the experiential, mobile and imaginative ways that people engage with their environments. In this conclusion I first make a series of observations concerning the character and implications of the approach I have developed in this book for working across disciplinary and other boundaries. I then draw together the findings of the earlier chapters to suggest how this approach might be harnessed to inform the ways we understand routes to a sustainable future.

BREAKING DOWN THE BOUNDARIES

To understand processes of sustainability theoretically, and to attempt to work towards these in applied research involves breaking down boundaries – between disciplines, between scholarly and applied and public research agendas, and between traditional research areas. This book has been an exercise in these processes. First, by opening up theoretical discussions to acknowledge the utility of approaches developed in anthropology, geography, sociology, cultural studies and philosophy as routes to abstract understandings of the experienced activities and environments encountered in ethnographic and digital research, we are able to see how different forms of abstraction bring us to different conclusions. Yet the existing literature has shown that these different approaches each bring us to relevant knowledge about processes of everyday life, activism and sustainability. Here I have suggested how we might work with a set of ideas drawn from these disciplines to form a coherent understanding of the experiential elements of these processes that moreover situates them within political processes.

Second, this book has crossed the fields of scholarly, applied and public research in several ways. The projects discussed in Chapters 4 and 5 about kitchen cleaning and laundry, respectively, were developed as applied consumer research projects. Yet here they have been engaged to make theoretical points, as well as to point to further issues of public and applied importance relating to questions around energy consumption. The project about the Cittaslow movement that was the main ethnographic basis for the discussions in Chapters 6 and 7 was initiated as a scholarly project seeking to understand local wellbeing. The research has led me in and out of scholarly and public spheres, to make theoretical contributions and to engage in public speaking about the movement. In this book both these elements of its implications are developed as I work with this ethnographic material theoretically to bring together phenomenological and political understandings of place, while simultaneously contributing to the analytical literature concerning sustainability in towns.

A third set of boundaries that I have suggested transgressing here are those between traditional research areas. I have argued that the inter-relationships between everyday life and activism might be further explored. This is not to say that these two fields of scholarship and analysis should be united in any essential sense, or that they always pertain to the same contexts as life is lived. Rather, my argument is that given that both fields are increasingly becoming important in the study of and move towards a sustainable society, it is important that we acknowledge their relationality. Everyday life has both historically and in a recent wave of publications been heralded as a key site for academic analysis. It has been posited as a domain of normative behaviours or conversely a site of resistance. It is at the centre of human existence, the essence of who we are and our location in the world. As scholars of everyday life have argued, it offers us a prism through which to study the world and it is moreover inextricably implicated in the making of the environments of which we are a part. In response to this existing body of literature in this book, I have argued for a resituating of everyday life, theoretically with attention to the relationship between practice and place, and substantively in terms of its relationship to activism and sustainability. It is perhaps no coincidence that this context of a renewed acknowledgement of the importance of understanding everyday life is emerging at the same time as a research focus on sustainability and climate change. In a contemporary context the quest for environmental and economic sustainability and scenarios where energy is saved and local economies thrive, the question of how activists and policy makers can mobilise everyday practices for these purposes is very pertinent. In Chapters 1–3, I have suggested that the kind of knowledge about the experience of everyday life that would be needed to understand how and why everyday processes might work towards sustainability could be developed through a focus on the sensory aesthetics of the everyday, on movement, the detail of practice and processes of creativity and an understanding of everyday life as always emplaced and also productive of place. This, however, creates a complicated conundrum, because while policies, the production of new technological possibilities and more can be owned or at least directed by key stakeholders involved with sustainability agendas, the ownership of the everyday is highly distributed: it belongs to all of us, collectively in one sense, but in another sense in a way that is highly individualised. This is not to say that all of our studies should be detailed analyses of a series of separate individuals and their uniqueness.

But rather that we need to account for the reality that many everyday life practices and places are experienced by individuals, sometimes alone, and in relation to their own biographies, memories and imaginations. Some of these can be analysed at a collective level, and there are certainly identifiable similarities and patterns in the ways certain people do things. We can also make some generalisations. Yet the contingency of practice and place is never obliterated by the possibility of making these more general statements and we should be careful not to let the possibility of generalising divert our attention from the diversity and potentialities of the everyday as it is lived. One future route to examining how everyday life and activism are intertwined is by attending to how the practices discussed in Chapters 4 and 5 can be explored by looking at how movements such as Slow Food seek to educate their members and others in alternative everyday practices. In Chapters 6, 7 and 8, I explored the relationship between everyday life and activism might be articulated in everyday neighbourhood contexts through town festivities and materialities and in relation to the Internet. Activism and everyday life are moreover intertwined in that activism can be an everyday practice. Working towards sustainability, whether as part of the work of an environmentalist movement or a policy agenda, inevitably depends to some extent on creating changes in the ways people can act in and experience the material and sensory environments of their everyday lives. As the example of the Cittaslow movement has shown, local policies and international movements can also become co-implicated. In a context where there is wide agreement across sectors that we need to work towards an environmentally sustainable future, it seems to me that it is crucial that we seek to understand the potential for producing sustainability at this interface – of everyday life, activism and policy – in its various manifestations.

Finally, as I highlighted in the introduction to this book, sustainability and thus everyday life and environmental activism are not simply concerns of the social sciences and humanities. Working towards a sustainable future is also a key concern for engineering and design disciplines and it is through collaborations across these areas that insights from the social sciences can have further impact.

ACCOUNTING FOR EXPERIENCE

Chapter by chapter I have explored a series of different contexts, from the kitchen to the Internet, through which the practices and places of everyday life are lived and constituted. These individual chapter studies do not themselves provide the answers to the questions about how we might make interventions. Yet they do suggest what kinds of research will lead to possible answers and what we might focus on in order to be able to have the knowledge that we would need to understand the ecologies of place that interventions in practice could become part of. In doing so I have proposed that it is through understanding these domains that we might further our knowledge about how a sustainable future might be achieved. It is my argument that such an understanding needs to be based on an analysis that appreciates the detail of everyday practice in private contexts alongside that of shared and public events and the global and publically accessible presentation of digital texts. My focus has also been on what might be broadly divided into three domains – the domestic, neighbourhood and urban. Some chapters have an almost exclusive focus on one or other of these but they also progressively overlap as we move through the book. Because the story this book tells is drawn from a range of separate but related projects; it is not intended as an empirical report on the current landscape of everyday life and activism in Britain. Moreover, it does not pretend to address a specific research or applied problem and produce a solution. Rather, I have undertaken an exploration in how theories of practice and place as open, contingent and mutually constituting might be mobilised in ways that enable a coherent understanding of everyday life and activism across a set of different types of locality or configuration of things, actions and environments. Before concluding, I draw together the findings of each chapter to suggest their implications for understanding sustainability in the context of everyday life and activist practice.

Initially I focused on the home as a context in which we might analyse the detail of practice and the making of sensory material localities. The two projects discussed in Chapters 4 and 5 were not directly concerned with sustainability when they were originally developed. Yet once I later began to research the Slow movement, which seeks to generate closer relationships between consumers and producers, bringing local products into people's homes, and to shift the ways people organise their lives, I realised that these were the sorts of domains that might be changed through slow lifestyles. Chapter 4 showed how the way people perform domestic tasks is personalised and tacit, depends on biography and memory and is part of the way identities are constituted. It is adapted to and creates particular ecologies of place. In this context living slowly as self-consciously voiced as an activist or in ways that are less explicitly informed by activist principles but yet engage with them has implications for the detail of everyday life in the home. Whereas Sue represented her cooking practices through a narrative of a slow-living identity, Nicola and Paul brought different modes of self-consciousness to the fore when (re) enacting their washing up. Making, performing and comprehending the kitchen is a multisensory and moral task – whether or not that morality or the principles which inform it pertain to a sustainability agenda. Moreover, while people might be aware of issues around the environment and energy consumption, engaging with these in practical and moral ways is complicated by other social, sensory and material elements of home. As I have shown in Chapter 5, understanding these as components of place and focusing on the flows of home enable us to comprehend how these different things come together to create specific domestic strategies. Chapter 5 outlined how the sensory home is created through a focus on laundry processes. Building on existing research that has identified laundry as a route through which to understand energy consumption in the home, I pushed this question further by asking what we might learn about this by analysing the routes that laundry takes through the home and the sensory aesthetics this involves. I suggested the choices people make (that lead them to consume energy) in their homes are contingent on a range of circumstances that are concerned with moralities, identities, social relationships and the physical layout of the home. Energy use and saving within the context of the laundry process in the sensory home became contradictory both between and within the narratives of different participants as we followed the routes of their laundry from the floor to the machine, the line, the dryer, the radiator, the clothes horse and the ironing board in front of the TV. In both of these chapters we see how the ways domestic tasks are performed are embedded in complex social, cultural, material, sensory, embodied biographical and memorial processes. They are performed in terms of their relationality with other components of the home. These are key domains in which everyday life is lived. They are therefore potentially the arenas upon which a sustainable future might at least partially depend. Chapters 4 and 5 thus demonstrate a set of principles about how and why people are able to sustain a particular sensory aesthetic in the home. If we take this as a starting point then it begins to lead us to a new understanding: if as I have argued in Chapter 2, learning and knowing is multisensory and the home can be understood as a multisensory environment, then what is important is what it feels like to be in the home. This goes beyond the focus on 'comfort' that is often used in the interdisciplinary energy studies literature. Rather, it suggests that a sustainable home needs to feel right – on a good number of levels – and that feeling right is what we are ultimately trying to achieve as we engage in a multitude of everyday domestic tasks. It directs us to start thinking further about the phenomenology of a sustainable world.

The following two Chapters, 6 and 7, indeed tell us more about what it might feel like to be in a sustainable place. These chapters focused more specifically on two contexts where sustainability agendas had informed the production of changes at two different levels. Chapter 6 focused on a community garden project to examine how a neighbourhood place which has been sustainable over time has been made. This project could indeed have been analysed as a successful case in the creation of a sustainable garden in an urban neighbourhood, and as an example of good practice. Yet my intention here is to go beyond its status as such a case study and to focus on how a theoretical analysis of this process can inform an understanding of sustainability. Thus to understand the processes through which the garden was made and became sustainable, it was crucial not only to examine the processes and practices through which committees formed and people carried out their work. Rather, it was essential to also examine both the experience of the garden and the invisible flows that at first sight one does not see circulating in the making of the garden. This approach opened up the possibility to understand the emotions and memories that are bound up in its making, the specificity of its composition and the processes of imagination that have been part of its production. Here we also saw how, while not all of these were immediately visible, the garden and its creation had been produced both through local people's imaginations, sentiments, labour and ideas, and using local materials, and from discourses and material sources that were distant from the garden itself and could be regarded as connected to global flows. This chapter shows how in this case the potentialities of human practices to grow into routine activities that produce and maintain a sustainable garden, were realised. Importantly, for participants the experience of being in the garden was central. David, who guided me around the site so many times, made sure to ask me if I had been able to imagine what it would be like before I had been in it. Crucially for the participants in the garden project, the field had felt wrong, not only physically because it was full of long, wet grass and looked derelict, but also because it engendered feelings of fear – that it might become more derelict or be filled with new buildings. Again we are led to consider the phenomenology of sustainable places as the field began to feel like a garden.

In Chapter 7 I discussed how a Cittaslow town was constituted through a series of activist practices and discourses which bound the local and its beyond together in various ways which were intended to work towards achieving a sustainable future. Here the analysis continued to draw from ethnographic experiences, and also focused in more closely on the roles played by practices of representation and their consumption. It considered how activist practices, informed by the discourses of a global urban social movement, can work towards transforming the possibilities for others to engage in sustainable practices. This chapter continued the reflections on how the local and global co-incide in place developed in Chapter 6. It also showed how an activist movement might generate possible ways of feeling and experiencing in a town, that are coherent with its sustainability agenda. Thus indicating how attention to the phenomenology of place can support our understanding of how sustainability is worked towards and experienced.

Chapter 8 focused on activist places online and explored how online materials can be understood as components of place that are, like the ethnographic contexts explored in the previous chapters, interwoven in complex ways. This chapter examined how the global mediated context is at the same time local and indeed that its local manifestations are both part of the way many people experience the everyday and are simultaneously framed by everyday life practices. I suggested that to understand digital activism the focus should shift to one that focuses on mediated contexts as components of place. Drawing from other existing work about media and activism as well as an analysis of the digital presence of the Cittaslow movement, I have argued that online materials might be understood as co-constituents of place that become interwoven both with other online content and with offline worlds. While my analysis in this chapter does not take an ethnographic focus on how users experience the web pages of the Cittaslow movement, my conclusions concur with the points I have made above. The phenomenology of the online experience, the ways we engage with software, narratives and representations and videos, open up possibilities for empathetic, sensory and affective experiences that invite us to go beyond the analysis of web pages in terms of their content or simply as representations. Therefore, while in a different context a semiotic content analysis of activist websites might serve a purpose, my point is rather different. In future research it would be important to attend to the possibilities that we have as users for individual and collective sensory, affective experiences of these different web platforms, both in terms of their mutual relationality and their relations to other elements of the everyday life place within which we experience them. As mobile digital media and a range of interrelated web platforms become increasingly ubiquitous in our lives, it is equally essential that we engage with these as part of the environments in which everyday life and activism are lived out. From the perspective of an approach that attends to the experiential as well as the networked and the political, the questions to ask therefore include: From what sets of relations is a sustainability agenda the outcome when it becomes manifested digitally through web platforms? And what does sustainability activism feel like when we experience it through digital media?

Therefore, as each of these chapters has shown, an approach to sustainability, activism and everyday life, approached through concepts of practice and place, might be consistently applied throughout a range of contexts. These continuities are crucial because they show us how attention to the experiential, the senses and to movement brings to the fore the very issues that we need to engage with when understanding how people can be implicated in a sustainable future. They also invite future research agendas which, rather than studying the home, neighbourhood, town and web platforms as if they were different places, would instead cut across these sites within the same programme of research.

TO CONCLUDE

In our contemporary world, sustainability, climate change and the reduction of carbon emissions, and the potential for activists, policy makers and governments to mobilise in relation to these issues, are increasingly important. Social scientists have a crucial role to play in this process. But in order for this to be effective, applied research in this area needs to be developed on the basis of critical and theoretically and methodologically coherent ways of understanding how everyday life practices and places are constituted and how they change.

If everyday life can be seen as the locus for a sustainable future, then it is only ethical for us, as those who live it (rather than as simply scholars who write about it), to be engaged in working towards it. As researchers we have the potential to inform interventions through detailed research that provides understandings of everyday practices and places. My argument in this book is that such research produced through participatory, collaborative and engaged methods that attend to and work with the practitioners of everyday life, provides routes to understanding the experiential dimensions of our relationships with other things, persons, localities and media that are so crucial in the decisions we take and actions we make. This means being immersed in some way in the world we are trying to understand, something that is in part inevitable in that we are already living everyday life, but that is also intentional in our seeking to implicate ourselves in the worlds and experiences of others as they are constituted and performed in different contexts.

BIBLIOGRAPHY

Amin, A. (2008) 'Collective culture and urban public space', *City* 12(1): 5–24.

Ardévol, E. (2012) 'Virtual/Visual Ethnography: methodological crossroads at the intersection of visual and Internet research', in Pink, S. (ed.) *Advances in Visual Methodology*. London: Sage.

Augé, M. (2008) *Non-Places: Introduction to an Anthropology of Supermodernity*. New York and London: Verso.

Baker, L.E. (2004) 'Tending cultural landscapes and food citizenship in Toronto's community gardens', *Geographical Review* 94(3): 305–25.

Barassi, V. (2010) 'Possibilities and ambivalences: the discursive power of online technologies and their impact on political action in Britain', in Trias, I. and Valls, A. (eds) *Anthropology Review: Dissent and Cultural Politics* 1: 4–14. Available online at http://issuu.com/ices/docs/ardac_may_2010 (accessed 19 July 2011).

Barnes, B. (2001) 'Practice as collective action theory', in Schatzki, T., Knorr-Cetina, K. and von Savigny, E. (eds) *The Practice Turn in Contemporary Theory*. London: Routledge.

Beer, W. (1983) *Househusbands: Men and Housework in American Families*. New York: Praeger Publishers.

Bell, D. and Jayne, M. (2007) *Small Cities: Urban Experience Beyond the Metropolis*. Oxford: Routledge.

Bell, D., Caplan, P. and Jahan Karim, W. (1993) *Gendered Fields: Women, Men and Ethnography*. London: Routledge.

Boellstorff, T. (2008) *Coming of Age in Second Life: An Anthropologist Explores the Virtually Human*. Princeton, NJ: Princeton University Press.

Booth, S. (1999) 'Reconstructing sexual geography: gender and space in changing Sicilian settlements', in Birdwell-Pheasant, D. and Lawrence-Zúñiga, D. (eds) *House Life-space: Place, Space and Family in Europe*. Oxford: Berg Publishers.

Bourdieu, P. (1977) *Outline of a Theory of Practice*. Cambridge: Cambridge University Press.

Bourdieu, P. (1987) *Choses dites*. Paris: Editions de Minuit.

Bourdieu, P. and Wacquant, L. (1992) *An Invitation to Reflexive Sociology*. Chicago, IL: University of Chicago Press.

Boyd, D. (2008) 'Can social network sites enable political action?', in Fine, A., Sifry, M., Rasiej, A. and Levy, J. (eds) *Rebooting America: Ideas for*

Redesigning American Democracy for the Internet Age, pp. 112–16. Creative Commons. Personal Democracy Press. Available online at http://rebooting.personaldemocracy.com (accessed 21 July 2011).

Bräuchler, B. and Postill, J. (eds) (2010) *Theorising Media and Practice.* Oxford: Berghahn.

Casey, E. (1996) 'How to get from space to place in a fairly short stretch of time', in Feld, S. and Basso, K. (eds) *Senses of Place.* Santa Fe, NM: School of American Research Press, pp. 13–52.

Casey, E. and Martens, L. (eds) (2007) *Gender and Consumption: Material Culture and the Commercialisation of Everyday Life.* Aldershot: Ashgate.

Castells, M. (1996) *The Rise of the Network Society.* Oxford: Blackwell.

Castells, M. (2000a) *The Information Age: Economy, Society and Culture,* updated edition. Oxford: Blackwell, 3 volumes.

Castells, M. (2000b) 'Materials for an exploratory theory of the network society', *British Journal of Sociology* 51(1): 5–24.

Castells, M. (2002 [2000]) 'Urban sociology in the twenty-first century', in Susser, I. (ed.) *The Castells Reader on Cities and Social Theory.* Oxford: Blackwell.

Castells, M. (2004) 'Informationalism, networks, and the network society: a theoretical blueprint', in Castells, M. (ed.) *The Network Society: A Cross-cultural Perspective,* Cheltenham, UK and Northampton, MA, USA: Edward Elgar Publishing.

Chadwick, A. (2006) *Internet Politics: States, Citizen, and New Communication Technologies.* Oxford: Oxford University Press.

Chevalier, S. (1995) 'The anthropology of an apparent banality: a comparative study', *Cambridge Anthropology* 18(3): 25–39.

Clark, D. (2003) *Urban World/Global City.* London: Routledge.

Clarke, A. (2001) 'The aesthetics of social aspiration', in Miller, D. (ed.) *Home Possessions.* Oxford: Berg.

Clifford, J. and Marcus, G. (1986) *Writing Culture: the Poetics and Politics of Ethnography.* Berkeley, CA: University of California Press.

Coffey, A. (1999) *The Ethnographic Self: Fieldwork and the Representation of Identity.* London: Sage.

Coleman, B. (2010) 'Ethnographic approaches to digital media', *Annual Review of Anthropology* 39: 487–505.

Coleman, S. and Collins, P. (2006) '"Being … where?": Performing fields on shifting grounds', in Coleman, S. and Collins, P. (eds) *Locating the Field: Space, Place and Context in Anthropology.* Oxford: Berg.

Couldry, N. (2004) 'Theorising media as practice', *Social Semiotics* 14(2): 115–32.

Couldry, N. and McCarthy, A. (2004) *MediaSpace: Place, Scale, and Culture in a Media Age.* London: Routledge.

Cresswell, T. (2002) 'Introduction: theorising place', *Thamyris/Intersecting: Place, Sex and Race* 9: 11–32.

Cresswell, T. (2003) 'Theorizing place, mobilizing place, placing mobility: the politics of representation in a globalized world', *Thamyris/Intersecting: Place, Sex and Race* 21: 11–31.

Cresswell T. (2010) 'Towards a politics of mobility', *Environment and Planning D: Society and Space* 28(1): 17–31.

Cytowic, R. (2010) 'Our hidden superpowers', *New Scientist* 24 April: 46.

de Certeau, M. (1984) *The Practice of Everyday Life*. Berkeley, CA: University of California Press.

de Certeau, M., Guard, L. and Mayol, P. (1998) *The Practice of Everyday Life, Volume 2: Living and Cooking*. Minneapolis, MO: University of Minnesota Press.

Degnen, C. (2009) 'On vegetable love: gardening, plants and people in the north of England', *Journal of the Royal Anthropological Institute* 15(1): 151–67.

Dicks, B., Soyinka, B. and Coffey, A. (2006) 'Multimodal ethnography', *Qualitative Research* 6(1): 77–96.

Downey, G. (2005) *Learning Capoeira: Lessons in Cunning from an Afro-Brazilian Art*. Oxford: Oxford University Press.

Downey, G. (2007) 'Seeing with a "sideways glance": visuomotor "knowing" and the plasticity of perception', in Harris, M. (ed.) *Ways of Knowing: New Approaches in the Anthropology of Experience and Learning*. Oxford: Berghahn.

Edwards, E., Gosden, C. and Phillips, R.B. (2006) Introduction to Edwards, E. Gosden, C. and Phillips, R.B. (eds) *Sensible Objects*. Oxford: Berg.

Farman, J. (2010) 'Mapping the digital empire: Google Earth and the process of postmodern cartography', *New Media and Society* 12(6): 869–88.

Feld, S. and Basso, K. (eds) (1996) *Senses of Place*. Santa Fe, NM: School of American Research Press.

Ferris, J., Norman, C. and Sempik, J. (2001) 'People, land and sustainability: community gardens and the social dimension of sustainable development', *Social Policy and Administration* 35(5): 559–68.

Fine, D.A. (2010) 'The culture of couples: a kaufmannesque sociology', *Contemporary Sociology: A Journal of Reviews* 39: 664–7.

Foote Whyte, W. (1993) *Street Corner Society: The Social Structure of an Italian Slum*, 4th edn. Chicago, IL: University of Chicago Press.

Fraser, E.D.G. (2002) 'Urban ecology in Bangkok, Thailand: community participation, urban agriculture and forestry', *Environments* 30(1): 37–49.

Gardiner, M. (2000) *Critiques of Everyday Life*. London: Routledge.

Gardiner, M. (2009) 'Book review: *Philosophizing the Everyday: Revolutionary Praxis and the Fate of Cultural Theory*, John Roberts (2006). London: Pluto. *Everyday Life: Theories and Practices From Surrealism to the Present*,

Michael Sheringham (2006). Oxford: Oxford University Press', *Space and Culture* 12: 383–8.

Geurts, K.L. (2002) *Culture and the Senses: Bodily Ways of Knowing in an African Community*. Berkely, CA: University of California Press.

Giard, L. (1998a) 'The nourishing arts', in De Certeau, M., Guard, L. and Mayol, P. (eds) *The Practice of Everyday Life, Volume 2: Living and Cooking*. Minneapolis, MO: University of Minnesota Press.

Giard, L. (1998b) 'The rules of the art', in De Certeau, M., Guard, L. and Mayol, P. (eds) *The Practice of Everyday Life, Volume 2: Living and Cooking*. Minneapolis, MO: University of Minnesota Press.

Giard, L. (1998c) 'Introduction to Volume 1: History of a Research Project', in De Certeau, M., Guard, L. and Mayol, P. (eds) *The Practice of Everyday Life, Volume 2: Living and Cooking*. Minneapolis, MO: University of Minnesota Press.

Gibson, J. (1966) *The Senses Considered as Perceptual Systems*. Boston, MA: Houghton Mifflin.

Gibson, J. (1979) *The Ecological Approach to Visual Perception*. Boston, MA: Houghton Mifflin.

Glover, T. D. (2004) 'Social capital in the lived experiences of community gardeners', *Leisure Sciences* 26(2): 143–62.

Goggin, G. (2006) *Cell Phone Culture: Mobile Technology in Everyday Life*. London: Routledge.

Gram-Hanssen, K. (2005) 'Teenage consumption of cleanliness', Danish Building Research Institute Department of Housing and Urban Renewal, presented at the conference, Kitchens and Bathrooms: Changing technologies, practices and social organisation – implications for sustainability, University of Manchester, UK.

Gram-Hanssen, K. (2008) 'Heat comfort and practice theory: understanding everyday routines of energy consumption', Chapter 1 in Proceedings: Referred Sessions I-II. Sustainable Consumption and Production: Framework for Action: 2nd Conference of the Sustainable Consumption Research Exchange (SCORE!) Network. Available online at http://www.score-network.org/files//24116_CF2_session_1-2.pdf (accessed 20 July 2011).

Grasseni, C. (2007) 'Communities of practice and forms of life: towards a rehabilitation of vision', in Harris, M. (ed.) *Ways of Knowing: New Approaches in the Anthropology of Experience and Learning*. Oxford: Berghahn.

Gray, J. (2003) 'Open spaces and dwelling places: being at home on hill farms in the Scottish borders', in Low, S.M. and Lawrence-Zuniga, D. (eds) *The Anthropology of Space and Place: Locating Culture*. Oxford: Blackwell.

Gupta, A. and Ferguson, J. (1997) *Culture, Power, Place: Explorations in Critical Anthropology*. Durham, NC: Duke University Press.

Guy, S. and Adams, M. (2007) 'Senses and the city', *Senses and Society* 2(2): 133–6.

Halkier, B., Katz-Gerro, T. and Martens, L. 'Applying practice theory to the study of consumption: (2011) theoretical and methodological considerations', *Journal of Consumer Culture* 11: 3-13.

Halstead, N., Hirsch, E. and Okley, J. (2008) *Knowing How to Know: Fieldwork and the Ethnographic Present*. Oxford: Berghahn.

Harris, M. (2007) 'Introduction: ways of knowing', in Harris, M. (ed.) *Ways of Knowing: New Approaches in the Anthropology of Experience and Learning*. Oxford: Berghahn.

Hecht, A. (2001) 'Home sweet home: tangible memories of an uprooted childhood', in Miller, D. (ed.) *Home Possessions*. Oxford: Berg.

Henning, A. (2005) 'Climate change and energy use: the role for anthropological research', *Anthropology Today* 21(3): 8–12.

Henning, A. (2006) *Can Qualitative Methods Support the Development of More Flexible and Energy Saving Thermal Comfort?* Available online at http://nceub.commoncense.info/uploads/Henning.pdf (accessed 20 July 2011).

Highmore, B. (2002) *Everyday Life and Cultural Theory*. London: Routledge.

Hine, C. (2000) *Virtual Ethnography*. London: Sage.

Hirsch, E. (1995) 'Landscape: between place and space', in Hirsch, E. and O'Hanlon, M. (eds) *The Anthropology of Landscape: Perspectives on Place and Space*. Oxford: Clarendon Press.

Howes, D. (ed.) (1991) *The Varieties of Sensory Experience: A Sourcebook in the Anthropology of the Senses*. Toronto: University of Toronto Press.

Howes, D. (2003) *Sensing Culture: Engaging the Senses in Culture and Social Theory*. Ann Arbour, MI: University of Michigan Press.

Howes, D. (ed.) (2005a) *Empire of the Senses: The Sensual Culture Reader*. Oxford: Berg.

Howes, D. (2005b) Introduction to D. Howes (ed.) *Empire of the Senses: The Sensory Culture Reader*. Oxford: Berg.

Hubbard, P., Kitchin, R. and Valentine, G. (2004) *Key Thinkers on Space and Place*. London: Sage.

Ingold, T. (2000) *The Perception of the Environment*. London: Routledge.

Ingold, T. (2007) *Lines: A Brief History*. London: Routledge.

Ingold, T. (2008) 'Bindings against boundaries: entanglements of life in an open world', *Environment and Planning A* 40: 1796–810.

Ingold, T. (2010a) 'Ways of mind-walking: reading, writing, painting', *Visual Studies* 25(1): 15–23.

Ingold, T. (2010b) 'Footprints through the weather-world: walking, breathing, knowing', *Journal of the Royal Anthropological Institute* 16: S121–S139.

Ingold, T. (2011) *Being Alive*. Oxford: Routledge.

Ingold, T. and Lee Vergunst, J. (eds) (2008) *Ways of Walking: Ethnography and Practice on Foot*. Aldershot: Ashgate.

James, A., Hockey, J. and Dawson, A. (1997) *After Writing Culture: Epistemology and Praxis in Contemporary Anthropology*. London: Routledge.

Juris, J.S. (2008) *Networking Futures*. Durham, NC: Duke University Press.

Kaufmann, J.C. (1998) *Dirty Linen: Couples as Seen Through Their Laundry*. Translated by Helen Alfrey. London: Middlesex University Press.

Knox, P. (2005) 'Creating ordinary places: slow cities in a fast world', *Journal of Urban Design* 10(1): 1–11.

Knox, P. and Mayer, H. (2009) *Small Town Sustainability*. Basel: Birkhäuser.

Kozinets, R. (2010) *Netnography: Doing Ethnographic Research Online*. London: Sage.

Kulick, D. and Willson, M. (eds) (1995) *Taboo: Sex, Identity and Erotic Subjectivity in Anthropological Fieldwork*. London: Routledge.

Kurtz, H. (2001) 'Building relationships, accessing resources: mobilizing social capital in community garden contexts', *Urban Geography* 22(7): 656–70.

Lapenta, F. (2011) 'Geomedia: on location-based media, the changing status of collective image production and the emergence of social navigation systems', *Visual Studies* 26(1): 14–24.

Lapenta, F. (2012) 'Geomedia based methods and visual research. Exploring the theoretical tenets of the localization and visualization of mediated social relations with direct visualization techniques', in Pink, S. (ed.) *Advances in Visual Methodology*. London: Sage.

Latour, B. (1992) 'Where are the missing masses? A sociology of a few mundane artifacts', in Bijker, W. and Law, J. (eds) *Shaping Technology/Building Society*. Cambridge, MA: MIT Press.

Law, L. (2005) 'Home cooking: Filipino women and geographies of the senses in Hong Kong', in Howes, D. (ed.) *Empire of the Senses: The Sensual Culture Reader*. Oxford: Berg.

Lee, J. and Ingold, T. (2006) 'Fieldwork on foot: perceiving, routing, socializing', in Coleman, S. and Collins, P. (eds) *Locating the Field: Space, Place and Context in Anthropology*. Oxford: Berg, pp. 67–86.

Leontidou, L. (2006) 'Urban social movements: from the "right to the city" to transnational spatialities and *flaneur* activists. Introduction', *City* 10(3): 259–68.

Löfgren, O. and Ehn, B. (2010) *The Secret World of Doing Nothing*. Berkeley, CA: University of California Press.

Low, S. and Lawrence-Zúñiga, D. (2003) 'Locating culture', in Low, S. and Lawrence-Zúñiga, D. (eds) *The Anthropology of Space and Place*. Oxford: Blackwell.

Lutzenhieser, L. and contributing authors (2009) *Behavioral Assumptions Underlying California Residential Sector Energy Efficiency Programs.* Available online at http://ciee-dev.eecs.berkeley.edu/energyeff/documents/ba_ee_res_wp.pdf (accessed 20 July 2011).

MacDougall, D. (1997) 'The visual in anthropology', in Banks, M. and Morphy, H. (eds) *Rethinking Visual Anthropology.* London: New Haven Press.

MacDougall, D. (1998) *Transcultural Cinema.* Princeton, NJ: Princeton University Press.

MacDougall, D. (2005) *The Corporeal Image: Film, Ethnography, and the Senses.* Princeton, NJ: Princeton University Press.

Malpass, A., Cloke, P., Barnett, C. and Clarke, N. (2007) 'Fairtrade urbanism? The politics of place beyond place in the Bristol fairtrade city campaign', *International Journal of Urban and Regional Research* 31(3):633–45.

Marchand, T.H.J. (2007) 'Crafting knowledge: the role of "parsing and production" in the communication of skill-based knowledge among masons', in Harris, M. (ed.) *Ways of Knowing: New Approaches in the Anthropology of Experience and Learning.* Oxford: Berghahn.

Marchand, T.H.J. (2010) 'Embodied cognition and communication: studies with British fine woodworkers', *Journal of the Royal Anthropological Institute* 16(s1): 100–20.

Marks, L. (2000) *The Skin of the Film.* Durham, NC: Duke University Press.

Martens, L. (2007) 'The visible and invisible: (de)regulation in contemporary cleaning practices', in Campkin, B. and Cox, R. (eds) *Dirt: New Geographies of Cleanliness and Contamination.* London: I.B. Tauris.

Martens, L. (2012) 'The politics and practices of looking: CCTV video and domestic kitchen practices', in Pink, S. (ed.) *Advances in Visual Methodology.* London: Sage.

Martens, L. and Scott, S. (2004) *Domestic Kitchen Practices: Routine, Reflexivity and Risk.* ESRC End of Award Report. Available online at http://www.esrc.ac.uk/my-esrc/grants/RES-000-22-0014/outputs/Read/414852c4-60a1-41dd-bda7-ef8c9883fd12 (accessed 21 July 2011).

Massey, D. (2005) *For Space.* London: Sage.

Massey, D. (2007) *World City.* Cambridge: Polity Press.

Mayer, H. and Knox, P. (2006) 'Slow cities: sustainable places in a fast world', *Journal of Urban Affairs* 28(4): 321–34.

Mayer, M. (2006) 'Manuel Castells' The City and the Grassroots', *International Journal of Urban and Regional Research* 30(1): 202–6.

Mayol, P. (1998) 'Living', in De Certeau, M., Guard, L. and Mayol, P. (eds) *The Practice of Everyday Life, Volume 2: Living and Cooking.* Minneapolis, MO: University of Minnesota Press.

Merleau-Ponty, M. (2002) *The Phenomenology of Perception*. London: Routledge.

Miah, A. and Rich, E. (2008) *The Medicalization of Cyberspace*. London: Routledge.

Miele, M. (2008) 'CittàSlow: producing slowness against the fast life', *Space and Polity* 12(1): 135–56.

Miller, D. (1988) 'Appropriating the State on the council estate', *Man* 23: 353–72.

Miller, D. (ed.) (1998) *Material Cultures*. London: Routledge.

Miller, D. (2001) 'Possessions', in Miller, D. (ed.) *Home Possessions*. Oxford: Berg.

Miller, D. (2011) *Tales from Facebook*. Cambridge: Polity.

Mirzoeff, N. (2002) 'The subject of visual culture', in Mirzeoff, N. (ed.) *The Visual Culture Reader*, 2nd edn. London: Routledge.

Mitchell, J.P. (2007) 'A fourth critic of the enlightenment: Michel de Certeau and the ethnography of subjectivity', *Social Anthropology* 15: 89–106.

Moran, J. (2005) *Reading the Everyday*. London: Routledge.

Nader, L. (2006) 'Rediscovering energy issues: a response to Harold Wilhite and Annette Henning', *Anthropology Today* 22(2): 22–3.

Nader, L. (2010) *The Energy Reader*. Malden, MA: Wiley Blackwell.

Napolitano, V. and Pratten, D. (2007) 'Certeau: Ethnography and the challenge of plurality', *Social Anthropology* 15(1): 1–12.

Newell, F. and Shams, L. (2007) 'New insights into multisensory perception', Guest editorial in *Perception*, special issue on 'Advances in multisensory research', 36: 1415–18.

O'Dell, T. (2010) *Spas and the Cultural Economy of Hospitality, Magic and the Senses*. Lund: Nordic Academic Press.

Oakley, A. (1974 [1985]) *The Sociology of Housework*. Oxford: Basil Blackwell.

Parkins, W. (2004) 'Out of time: fast subjects and slow living', *Time and Society* 13(2–3): 363–82.

Parkins, W and Craig, G. (2006) *Slow Living*. Oxford: Berg.

Petridou, E. (2001) 'The taste of home', in Miller, D. (ed.) *Home Possessions*. Oxford: Berg.

Petrini, C. (2001) *Slow Food: The Case for Taste*. New York: Columbia University Press.

Petrini, C. (2007) *Slow Food Nation: Why Our Food Should be Good, Clean and Fair*. New York: Rizzoli ex libris.

Pink, S. (2004) *Home Truths: Gender, Domestic Objects and Everyday Life*. Oxford: Berg.

Pink, S. (2005) 'Dirty laundry: everyday practice, sensory engagement and the constitution of identity', *Social Anthropology* 13(3): 275–90.

Pink, S. (2006) *The Future of Visual Anthropology*. London: Routledge.

Pink, S. (2007a) *Doing Visual Ethnography*. London: Sage.

Pink, S. (ed.) (2007b) *Visual Interventions*. Oxford: Berghahn.

Pink, S. (2007c) 'Sensing Cittàslow: slow living and the constitution of the sensory city', *Sense and Society* 2(1): 59–77.

Pink, S. (2007d) 'The sensory home as a site of consumption: everyday laundry practices and the production of gender', in Casey, E. and Martens, L. (eds) *Gender and Consumption: Material Culture and the Commercialisation of Everyday Life*. Aldershot: Ashgate Press.

Pink, S. (2007e) 'Walking with video', *Visual Studies* 22(3): 240–2.

Pink, S. (2008a) 'Sense and sustainability: the case of the slow city movement', *Local Environment* 13: 95–106.

Pink, S. (2008b) 'Re-thinking contemporary activism: from community to emplaced sociality', *Ethnos* 73(2): 163–88.

Pink, S. (2008c) 'Analysing visual experience', in Pickering, M. (ed.) *Research Methods in Cultural Studies*. Edinburgh: Edinburgh University Press.

Pink, S. (2009a) *Doing Sensory Ethnography*. London: Sage.

Pink, S. (2009b) 'Urban social movements and small places', *City* 13(4): 451–65.

Pink, S. (2010) 'The future of sensory anthropology/the anthropology of the senses', *Social Anthropology* 18(3): 331–3.

Pink, S. (2011a) 'Sensory digital photography: re-thinking "moving" and the image', *Visual Studies* 26(1): 4–13.

Pink, S. (2011b) 'Amateur documents?: amateur photographic practice, collective representation and the constitution of place in UK slow cities', *Visual Studies* 26(2): 92–101.

Pink, S. (2011c) 'Multi-modality and multi-sensoriality and ethnographic knowing: or can social semiotics be reconciled with the phenomenology of perception and knowing in practice', *Qualitative Research* 11(3): 261–76.

Pink, S. (2011d) 'Ethnography of the invisible: how to "see" domestic and human energy', *Ethnologia Europaea: Journal of European Ethnology* 41(1): 117–28.

Pink, S. (2012) 'Visual ethnography and the internet: visuality, virtuality and the spatial turn', in Pink, S. (ed.) *Advances in Visual Methodology*. London: Sage.

Postill, J. (2008) 'Localising the internet beyond communities and networks', *New Media and Society* 10(3): 413–31.

Postill, J. (2010) 'Introduction: theorising media and practice', in Bräuchler, B. and Postill, J. (eds) *Theorising Media and Practice*. Oxford: Berghahn.

Postill, J. (2011) *Localizing the Internet: An Anthropological Account*. Oxford: Berghahn.

Reckwitz, A. (2002) 'Towards a theory of social practices: a development in culturalist theorizing', *European Journal of Social Theory* 5(2): 243–63.

Rodaway, P. (1994) *Sensuous Geographies: Body, Sense and Place*. London: Routledge.

Rouch, J. (2003[1973]) 'The camera and man' in S. Field (ed.) *Cine-Ethnography Jean Rouch*. London: University of Minnesota Press.

Rouch, J. and Morin, E. (dir.) (1961) *Chronique d'un été*. Paris: Argos Films.

Sahakian, M.D. (2010) 'Understanding household energy consumption patterns: when "west is best" in Metro Manila', *Energy Policy* 39(2): 596–602.

Schatzki, T. (1996) *Social Practices: A Wittgensteinian Approach to Human Activity and the Social*. Cambridge: Cambridge University Press.

Schatzki, T. (2001) 'Introduction: practice theory', in Schatzki, T., Knorr-Cetina, K. and von Savigny, E. (eds) *The Practice Turn in Contemporary Theory*. London: Routledge.

Schatzki, T., Knorr-Cetina, K. and von Savigny, E. (eds) (2001) *The Practice Turn in Contemporary Theory*. London: Routledge.

Schneider, A. and Wright, C. (eds) (2005) *Contemporary Art and Anthropology*. Oxford: Berg.

Schneider, A. and Wright, C. (eds) (2010) *Between Art and Anthropology*. Oxford: Berg.

Seremetakis, N. (1994) *The Senses Still: Perception and Memory as Material Culture in Modernity*. Chicago, IL: University of Chicago Press.

Sheringham, M. (2006) *Everyday Life: Theories and Practices from Surrealism to the Present*. Oxford: Oxford University Press.

Shove, E. (2003) *Comfort, Cleanliness and Convenience*. Oxford: Berg.

Shove, E., Watson, M., Ingram, J. and Hand, M. (2007) *The Design of Everyday Life*. Oxford: Berg.

Shove, E., Trentmann, T. and Wilk, R. (eds) (2009) *Time, Consumption and Everyday Life: Practice, Materiality and Culture*. Oxford: Berg.

Simonsen, K. (2007) 'Practice, spatiality and embodied emotions: an outline of a geography of practice', *Human Affairs* 17: 168–81. Available online at http://versita.metapress.com/content/w15n2x52444u0112/fulltext.pdf (accessed 12 January 2011).

Stoller, P. (1989) *The Taste of Ethnographic Things: The Senses in Ethnography*. Philadelphia, PA: University of Philadelphia Press.

Stoller, P. (1997) *Sensuous Scholarship*. Philadelphia, PA: University of Pennsylvania Press.

Sutton, D. (2006) 'Cooking skill, the senses, and memory: the fate of practical knowledge', in Edwards, E., Gosden, C. and Phillips, R.B. (eds) *Sensible Objects*. Oxford: Berg.

Tacchi, J. (1998) 'Radio texture: between self and others', in Miller, D. (ed.) *Material Cultures*. London: Routledge.

Thrift, N.J. (2008) *Non-representational Theory: Space, Politics, Affect*. London: Routledge.

Tilley, C. (2006) 'The sensory dimensions of gardening', *Senses and Society* 1(3): 311–30.

Tomlinson, J. (2007) *The Culture of Speed: The Coming of Immediacy*. London: Sage.

Tuan, Yi-Fu (1993) *Passing Strange and Wonderful: Aesthetics, Nature, and Culture*. Washington, DC: Island Press, Shearwater Books.

Uricchio, W. (2011) 'The algorithmic turn: photosynth, augmented reality and the changing implications of the image', *Visual Studies* 26(1): 25-35.

Wakefield, S., Yeudall, F., Taron, C., Reynolds, J. and Skinner, A. (2007) 'Growing urban health: community gardening in South-East Toronto', *Health Promotion International* 22(2): 92–101.

Warde, A. (2005) 'Consumption and theories of practice', *Journal of Consumer Culture* 5(2): 131–53.

Wenger, E. (1998) *Communities of Practice: Learning, Meaning, and Identity*. Cambridge: Cambridge University Press.

Wilhite, H. (2005) 'Why energy needs anthropology', *Anthropology Today* 21(3): 1–2.

Wilhite, H. (2008) *Consumption and the Transformation of Everyday Life*. Basingstoke: Palgrave.

Wilhite, H., Nakagami, H., Masuda, T., Yamaga, Y. and Haneda, H. (1996) 'A cross-cultural analysis of household energy-use behavior in Japan and Norway', *Energy Policy* 24(9): 795–803.

Wilk, R.R. (n.d.) *Culture and Energy Consumption*. Available online at http://indiana.academia.edu/RichardWilk/Papers/10894/Culture_and_Energy_Consumption (accessed 20 July 2011).

Wills, J., Chinemana, F. and Rudolph, M. (2010) 'Growing or connecting? An urban food garden in Johannesburg', *Health Promotion International* 25(1): 33–41.

Wynn Kirby, P. (2009) *Boundless Worlds: An Anthropological Approach to Movement*. Oxford: Berghahn.

INDEX